Loving Your Life

International Acclaim

"*Loving Your Life* offers a genuinely kind attitude towards life and art. The image of a colour-filled brush emerges in one's mind's eye. The brush playfully caresses the totality of everyday experience, touching the sad, grieving, and unloved aspects of life. Combining the principles of attraction with the honesty of her introspection, Elke Scholz transforms hitherto lofty mainstream understandings into grounded spirituality that we can live, dance, and paint by."
— Bihter Yasemin Adali, MA, Expressive Arts Therapist and Founding Member, Arts Psychotherapies Association, Istanbul, Turkey

"This collection contains a wealth of innovative ideas for involving children and adults in therapy sessions. The interventions are classified into sections that therapists can easily select and apply. A valuable resource for mental health professionals who work in this field. Elke shows how love and an open heart give us access to creative living."
— Vered Zur, MA, CAGS, Director of Expressive Arts, Ireland

"Elke Scholz writes with a lively and clear style that anyone can understand. Every word of it comes from the heart. I recommend her book to artists, therapists, and to anyone who wants to live an authentic, creative life."
— Prof. Tom McLaughlin, Appalachian University, Boone, North Carolina

"Throughout *Loving Your Life*, Elke safely, joyfully, and artistically guides you into your path not taken . . . the path that sometimes we skip . . . the path to our heart."
— Joana Fins Faria, Expressive Arts Therapist, Portugal

"There are countless ways in the world and in communication with other people to meet oneself. And there are just as many ways to communicate one's experiences to others so that they can have their own experiences. It is this diversity that has to be esteemed and cherished, because it is an expression of the uniqueness of every human being, and, ultimately, of every moment. Elke Scholz pioneers here an artistic way — and I hope the book that many people are so excited about will help them to achieve positive experiences for themselves."
— Prof. Dr. Jürgen Kriz, Dept. of Psychology, Psychotherapy and Clinical Psychology, Universität Osnabrück, Germany

"I am convinced that we can liberate many hidden traumas by giving our heart a voice, by expressing ourselves through art . . . your book is authentic and reflects what you live."

Gabriela Hennig, Peru

"Reading the book *Loving Your Life* changed my life, my way of looking at things, nature, and human beings; being aware of myself, my body, and of being creative. I carried the book with me over a long time . . . I came closer to my creativity . . . I love the 'six steps' in the teachers' notes. I would recommend this book to many people around me—professionals and clients—who are looking for a source of inspiration and development of self."

Liselotte Dietrich, MA EXAT, Urnäsch, Hungary, and Switzerland

"I highly recommend [this book] to all creative arts therapists in particular, because it reminds us to reignite that creative process in us, the core reason why we became arts therapists!"

Daniel A. Hyams, London, England

"I believe her book is an offering to the world, to those willing to search inside, grow, heal, look for meaning. She takes us on a ride through the world of the expressive arts, while making us feel safe and using her life experience and deep wisdom to guide us into trying a healthy and more meaningful way of living."

Alina Tomsa, Romania

"*Loving Your Life* is an extraordinary book, written by an extraordinary woman. Elke Scholz offers us hope as she gently teaches us how to explore individual freedom of expression through art making, and how to live our lives to the fullest. A truly great, resonant, and inspirational read for all ages!"

Cheryl Cooper, Author of Come Looking for Me

"*Loving Your Life* is born out of a place of deepening. An extended second edition can only mean an additional gift of an artful and heartful journey through the words of this writer, artist, and expressive arts therapist."

Taraneh Erfan King, MA, RCC, Registered Clinical Counsellor and Expressive Arts Therapist, Vancouver, Canada

"As an art therapist, I am seduced by this wonderful book to play, explore, experiment, and share with my clients. Elke draws its practical exercises from everyday life. They are of great aesthetic value and inspiration for living."

Rut Tschofen, MA, Switzerland

Loving Your Life

Elke Scholz

Foreword by **Kate Donohue**
A grandmother of Expressive Arts Therapy

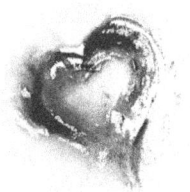

An illustrated how-to book on becoming who you are and loving it, through passionate, creative living

THIRD EDITION

Published by
The Artist's Reply

ISBN 978-0-9736023-4-0 (pbk)
ISBN 978-0-9736023-6-4 (epub)
ISBN 978-09736023-5-7 (mobi)

Copyright © Elke Scholz, 2004, 2013, 2016

Cover art and illustrations: Elke Scholz
Design: Magdalene Carson, New Leaf Publication Design
Back cover photo of Elke Scholz: Brandon Lemesurier

All rights reserved. No part of this book may be reproduced, stored in a retrieval system, or transmitted in any form or by any means without the prior written permission of the publisher or, in case of photocopying or other reprographic copying, a licence from Access Copyright (The Canadian Copyright Licensing Agency). For permissions, please visit their website: www.accesscopyright.ca

Cataloguing in Publication data available from Library and Archives Canada

DISCLAIMER

The author of this book does not dispense medical advice or prescribe the use of any technique as a form of treatment for physical, emotional, mental or medical problems without the advice of a physician, either directly or indirectly. The intent of the author is to offer only general information in a general nature to help you in your exploration for spiritual and emotional well being. In the event you use any of this information for yourself or others, the author and publisher assume no responsibility for your actions.

For my children, Alec and Emma,
and for all the youth of the world:
They are our future.

Contents

Foreword *ix*
Acknowledgments *xi*
Introduction: First Edition *xiii*
Introduction: Second Edition *xv*
Introduction: Third Edition *xx*
How to Use This Book *xxi*

one **THE BEGINNING** *1*
The Breath of Life *3*
Thinking about time *11*
The power of thought *16*
Choosing your state of mind *20*
Freeing your imagination *24*
Your spiritual self *26*
Defining your purpose *27*

two **CLEAR HEARING** *31*
Intuitive listening *33*
Journal writing —— healing words *42*
Sound awareness *46*
Music *47*

three **CHALLENGE AND CHANGE** *55*
About change *57*
The notion of "mistakes" *65*
Stumbling blocks *66*
The many aspects of stress and creativity *82*
Taking charge of your thoughts *93*
Communicating mindfully with others *96*

four **BUILDING A MOUNTAIN** *103*
Knowing yourself *105*
Understanding your emotions *121*

five **CREATIVITY LOOKS LIKE THIS** *135*
Being creative *137*
Resisting creativity *140*
Stimulating your creative energy *142*
Stimulating your senses *144*
Changing your channels *146*

six   **THE ARTS EXPERIENCE**   *149*
        Experiencing art   *151*
        Venturing into art   *155*
        Art provokes beneficial change   *157*
        Seeing life differently   *160*
        Common misconceptions about art   *162*
        Preparing for your artistic journey   *164*
        Developing personal vision and unique style   *173*
        The unknown   *176*
        An invitation to draw   *177*
        Doing art together   *190*
        Being in the moment   *192*

seven   **EMBRACING DEATH, EMBRACING LIFE**   *195*
        Embracing death   *197*
        Fear of death   *199*
        Knowing that you are going to die   *206*
        Embracing grief and loss   *210*
        How do children grieve?   *217*

eight   **MAPPING YOUR JOURNEY**   *225*
        Becoming who you are   *227*
        Continue to balance and love life   *228*
        Strengthening inner and outer happiness   *230*
        Daily Practice   *231*
        Outer Happiness   *238*
        Environment   *239*
        Music, entertainment, reading   *240*
        Choose and do what works best for you   *241*

        Resources and References   *245*
        About the Author   *251*

Foreword

Elke Scholz has cooked up a compassionate, caring and creative brew in this fine book instructing the reader on how to live what you love. She uses her own experience and visual and poetic images, as well sound clinical and expressive arts theory and wisdom, to portray a vivid, vibrant path dedicated to the arts as a means to designing a fuller, richer life.

Her dedication to healing and the arts led her to join the board of the International Expressive Arts Therapy Association (IEATA), and take on a leadership role in the field as co-chair of the Artist's Committee. It was under these circumstances I came to know and respect Elke. We met at the Hong Kong conference of IEATA and connected on a deeply personal and professional leadership basis. As one of the founding board members of IEATA, I wanted to help Elke feel comfortable in her new role. I learned Elke was an accomplished writer, artist, poet, trained and registered psychotherapist, as well as a registered expressive arts educator/consultant (REACE) and, most importantly, a very soulful and sincere woman. Later, while teaching in Winnipeg, Canada, Elke attended one of my workshops. I could sense in the group she was a leader with a compassionate heart, and I witnessed her deeply moving paintings, with their impressionistic nature themes, which felt to me like dream material reflecting the emotion and beauty of nature that calls us back to our roots to seek healing.

In reflecting on this book's format, one sees Elke as a woman who "walks her talk", starting with her own story on how the arts changed her life. She employs her own artwork throughout the book as an illumination of her experience and training. While similar to *The Artists' Way* in terms of offering a structure to help with one's own explorations, it is substantially more soulful, and offers a multi-arts approach Elke learned at the European Graduate School (EGS).

As a Jungian expressive arts psychologist in practice for more than thirty years in Northern California, I deeply appreciate Elke's intuitive skills, starting from a foundation of breath, body and the receptive arts: listening to bodily gestures such as smiling, music, mindfulness, and selecting visual images that have emotional meaning to the person, each of which change one's neurochemistry. She also guides the reader through actively listening to their body, mind and soul. Then she introduces the idea of a creative practice, using one's imagination to change one's life. Living the great quote by Albert Einstein, "imagination is more important than intelligence", she joins the ideas of physics and spirituality through the lens of the creative process, even addressing the concept of resisting the arts and change. Elke intuitively embodies Jung's ideas of the importance of one's internal world to discover the self/Self as our guide to living a life we can love. Resisting the new age conceit that all is "in the light", she delves into grief and loss and one's own death as teachers worthy of our attention. She suggests the best learning occurs when we burrow into the unknown, including the parts of ourselves we are afraid of, à la Jung's shadow.

An excellent book for the layperson, *Loving Your Life* is a step-by-step approach that first explores a concept, followed by Elke's own personal experience and discoveries, then provides a process for the reader to investigate, and even offers what one might expect as an outcome. Each chapter suggests a creative practice and also urges journaling to deepen one's understanding of the symbolic function — or meaning — for your life and its transformation. Elke believes, similarly to Carl Jung, Otto Rank, Carl Rogers and Paolo Knill, that deep inside of us we have a wealth of creativity, intuition and knowledge. Her processes bring these internal gifts and resources to consciousness and light, enabling the reader to acknowledge them and follow their own deep, quiet voice and live a more fulfilling existence, attuned with their body, mind and soul. I would recommend this book wholeheartedly to my clients, students and trainees, as well as the general public.

Kate T. Donohue, Ph.D., REAT is licensed psychologist with a registered Jungian expressive arts therapy orientation (REAT) for thirty-five years. She was a co-founder board member of the International Association of Expressive Arts Therapy (IEATA) and has served in many roles, chair of the professional standards committee, executive co-chair, twice as conference co-chair in San Francisco and Hong Kong, and is now honorary advisor to the organization. Along with Jack Weller and Sanjen Miedzinski, she was a founding core faculty member of the Expressive Arts Therapy Department at the California Institute of Integral Studies (CIIS). Currently Kate is an international trainer of Jungian oriented expressive arts therapy through Asia and Ghana, Africa, and is a therapist, supervisor and author internationally. Her latest passion is conducting expressive arts cultural journeys, exploring the indigenous roots of expressive arts in Ghana and Southern India. Kate loves dance, drama and painting, and loves being with her redwood trees in her new home in Fort Bragg, California.

Acknowledgments

I appreciate all my students and clients, my fellow companions on this creative life journey. Their questions and successes have prompted many ideas for this book. Listening to their suggestions and encouragement has forged the contents.

Special thanks to all my teachers and mentors at Sir Sandford Fleming College's Haliburton School of The Arts, International School of Interdisciplinary Studies, CREATE Institute,(Centre for Expressive Arts Therapy Education) known as CANADA's Creative Integrative Arts Therapy Training Program, and the European Graduate School (EGS) in Saas Fee, Switzerland.

Thank you to Lilo Dietrich for reviewing the book as a supervisor and fellow colleague at EGS, and Dr. Tom McLaughlin, Creative English professor at Appalachian State University, Boone, North Carolina, for reviewing and giving fresh eyes to the nuances of word meanings for readers.

Special thanks to Melanie Nesbitt, my thesis advisor and reviewer, for helping me integrate my Expressive Arts Learning and the first into the second edition of this book.

Special thanks to Gayle Barnet for helping me push my own boundaries in writing about death.

Special thanks to our local high schools for keeping the door open for the many youth programs.

I am also grateful to my daily spiritual practice for it is the foundation of my life and the principles in this book.

Thank you to all my friends and family for understanding my focus on this enormous project. Thanks Alec and Emma for supporting your busy mom.

Stillness

When I walk in the woods or sit by a river I feel perfect,
that my life is perfect, that everything is perfect
right now. I look at the trees that grow slowly,
over time, crooked, asymmetrical, storm wounds and all,
yet balanced. Balanced with each other, other trees,
some rotten, still feeding, functioning,
providing life support, all vital, all important, all different.
The trees didn't grow over one night, or one week,
yet in their own time have grown strong, perfect.
Crooked, holy, peeling bark, fungus, natural beauty
I feel beautiful in the woods, with the fallen leaves
and sweet earthy smells. There is no judgment,
on how I look, on what I say,
no judgment on the shape of my body, what I am,
how I walk, or if I walk.
I can just be,
nothing else and everything else.

I am enough.

Introduction: First Edition

Love your life! Feel great! Be happy! We deserve to live the best life possible.

This book is not about fixing or changing who you are. How do you increase your awareness of yourself and your surroundings? How do you make wise choices that best enrich your life so you can fully live and enjoy it? What does self-care look like?

This book is a safe beginning for individuals just starting their journey to fuller self-awareness and creativity. It also provides support and stimulation for creative individuals already living their dream.

What I know comes from my own life experience and the experiences of my students and clients as we have learned through practising the arts and integrating body/brain learning. These insights I share in my workshops and in this book. Combining the arts with awareness techniques and living skills can produce powerful, life-changing results.

I believe that as we grow up, many of us develop blocks to our awareness, sensitivity, perception, intelligence, and capacity for happiness. These blocks can cloud, confuse, mask, and/or inhibit hearing our wise, intuitive inner voice and body intelligence, making it difficult to choose what's best for us and those around us.

We don't need to understand, label, analyze, or share all these blocks to transform them into learning tools that can assist us in our daily living. Studies show that when feelings and emotions are expressed, they become unblocked. They transform and evolve. Having feelings and emotions witnessed makes the experience stronger and more transformative.

The arts will stimulate the neural pathways in your brain with new perspectives.

The arts offer us a non-verbal and non-threatening form of self-expression, allowing us to translate and transform feelings and emotions without judgment. We can feel relaxed, open, energized, and receptive to learning. And we often find hidden strengths and resources.

As a child, I knew anything was possible, and knowing that made it true. As I grew older, I started doubting the miracles of life, the awesome positive energy and power in our universe. I began to ration my wishes, hopes, and dreams. Looking back, I also sabotaged some of those dreams. As I grew to understand what was happening and what I was and wasn't doing, I gradually came back to the knowing of my childhood, to knowing that the source of creation was within me, that we are all possibilities, that we are creative already.

With clarity of mind, body, and spirit, we can access so many possibilities. I experience, see, and live this most of my moments and I want to share it in a simple, enjoyable way that I believe is true to our human nature.

The challenge is to communicate this abstract, non-linear thinking, to put into words and action the non-verbal concepts. In the "doing" of creative non-verbal actions, we can pull away barriers and blocks so we can access our true potential, our true happiness. We can observe our life stories in art—we can build and strengthen our resources.

In this book, I refer to many forms of non-verbal communication, including music, dance, and, most frequently, drawing. Drawing helps us to develop perception skills, which in turn serve as a foundation for visual communication. Learning to draw is to visual communication what learning to write is to verbal communication. Drawing is accessible, economical, and instinctive. It opens our eyes. After drawing, we cannot help but see our world differently.

This book is a guide to "doing," finding, accessing, and communicating what we already know deep inside us. The doing brings to surface the awareness, thoughts, wants, desires, ability, and power that got buried along the way. In the doing, we access our own truth, and that will help us find our own way to live well and be absolutely happy.

Introduction: Second Edition

Since self-publishing the first edition of this book in 2004, I have been welcomed into the Expressive Arts Community internationally. I realized that I had been practising expressive arts as an adult and a facilitator for over thirty years. These concepts have always made sense to me, and the proof is in the continuing successes of my students, my clients, and myself.

In 2006, I graduated from the Expressive Arts program at Sir Sandford Fleming College, Haliburton, Ontario; in 2009, I graduated from a three-year intensive program at a private college, ISIS Canada, in Toronto, Ontario, in Expressive Arts Therapy. In 2011, I successfully completed the Masters level for Expressive Arts Therapy at European Graduate School (EGS), Saas Fee Campus, Switzerland.

Since 2007, this writer has practised EXA therapy on private clients and youth groups for hospice, the local boards of education, and the District of Muskoka. With this accumulated Expressive Arts experience and studies, I am reshaping the book *Loving Your Life* for a revised second edition.

I am very pleased to say that the book continues to stand strong on supporting individual creativity and supporting self-care. This edition includes some expressive arts terms.

In some of the creative practices, I have offered additional exercises to further the creative experience.

I have also added a chapter on dying. Death is a natural part of our life and an important part of loving life. In my experience, our society does not manage death and loss well, which I address in chapter seven.

The resources and reference sections have been expanded to reflect my continuing research.

The purpose of these subtle changes for this already successful, well-received book is to enhance the reader's experience by being more positive; bringing more hope; offering more varied art discipline processes; and offering more reference materials, more community, and more of the therapeutic model.

How have I changed since my formal training?

Since my training, five major things have shifted for me in my personal and professional life, all of which have resulted in a more harmonious, fuller life, filled with growing synchronicities:

I am more comfortable with the unknown.

I am stronger in my intuitive sense.

I can sit in the swamp with myself and others.

I am more present.

I am more confident.

When I began EXA, I remember how I detested not knowing the plan or routine ahead of time. I had anxiety over new routines and new ventures. As much as EXA and this education was a dream come true, my anxiety level was very high. I re-mortgaged my house, re-budgeted my finances, rented out my son's former room, and set up a local practicum before I was interviewed for my acceptance by the ISIS college. That was the easy part. Emotionally and physically, my stomach was in knots, and inside I was shaky.

I could manage only one semester at a time. Even though very resistant, I grew more comfortable in not knowing what lay ahead: of a class, travel, my work, or a session with a client. This did not happen overnight, and I would not have believed I could change that much—even though at one time I had wished I could.

All the institutions and practices at ISIS strengthened our sensitivity, our intuition, and our urges, which are so important to this work and to living well. I rely on my intuition and urges in my daily life, and especially in my private practice.

As much as I plan my sessions and get ready, I am open to what the client brings. It is his or her day and time. There are infinite possibilities in what can be brought forward, and I rely on my intuition as to what to do next. The training has helped me give in to the moment, to be open to, and curious about, what is brought forward.

Time and daily practice are essential for me. This regular self-care is an ongoing process; although it used to feel laborious, it now feels more like self-love.

I pride myself as a positive thinker and an action-oriented person. I practise the principles of attraction. A few years ago, my daughter finally burst out in an emotional, crying, gut-wrenching heap of misery. She had been holding back her anger and grief because, she said, she did not want to feel them in case she attracted more of this deep pain. I was taken aback. Stunned, I had to rethink positive thinking, realistic thinking, and authentic feeling. How do I sit with these dark, sad, yukky feelings in a healthy way and not attract more to myself? How and when are unpleasant emotions useful?

This concept and question is very important, as it affects how I live my life, guide my children, and work in my practice of helping others—especially this book.

I have learned to not be afraid to sit in chaos, deep grief, raging anger, deep sadness, and angst-filled questions. I've learned that the intensity cannot sustain itself and can move. Emotions have qualities; they exist, whether useful or not.

What I am learning is how to keep the feelings moving. It's when feelings are stuffed away and suppressed that they fester, grow, and attract more of the same and invite disease. It is hard to sit with someone in his or her swamp; however, it is a journey and a work that has significant rewards. It is also hard not to simply solve things and to sit with more questions—although with EXA, I can.

Prior to my EXA learning and EXA work, I had a horrible fear of death. Working with death and grief has helped me accept my own death and that of others. In my humanness, I still feel the loss of life through death. In accepting death, life has become even more precious and more wondrous.

I have practised and studied meditation for many years. I live in nature as much as I can. I begin my day with gratitude, prayer, meditation, and a long walk in the woods along the river. All this maintenance helps ground and calm me. EXA has emphasized my own self-care.

My EXA training has given me a way to express myself with the arts in an organized way. I can bring myself and/or a situation to a session and am able to "harvest" the new stimulation/ideas my brain has experienced by artistic expression. It's given me a way to understand non-verbal sensations and to get them outside myself by means of art. With this practice, I do this non-verbally or verbally.

EXA has fast-forwarded moving through personal layers of healing—like peeling the skin of an onion—to where I am now. I feel more authentic and grounded in all respects. I feel my life makes a little bit of sense now and again. I live my life purpose. Many days I feel satisfied.

My life is the best it has ever been, and I am the happiest I have ever been; and this I share with the reader of this book.

What Are the Expressive Arts?

Life and art are connected in many metaphorical ways and levels. Expressive Arts invites us to explore ourselves and our senses by art-making. The arts allow us to freely express ourselves outside the boundaries of language.

In a strong verbal world, the arts offer a wealth of non-verbal intelligence, helping to strengthen our creative power and deepen our relationship with life. The arts stimulate the brain in new ways of thinking. You are most knowledgeable of your own life. Your expressions in art are most meaningful to you and your situation.

In the doing of Expressive Arts, we can build on our inner wisdom and resilience. This act of doing could be an act of moving from being stuck.

Expressive Arts can be described as integrating sensory modalities such as seeing, hearing, touching, and using different disciplines such as imagery, breathing, painting, drawing, sculpture, movement, music, play, drama, poetry, and/or journalling (e.g., writing a phrase in response to a painting). Technical experience in modalities is not necessary, as the goal is to "express" an emotion, self, or situation. It is not to create an art piece; it is a way to shape an image for a new perspective. The client requires no formal art training. It is an invitation for self-expression and self-exploration.

Moving from modality to modality in the different disciplines helps us move through a situation or issue.

> *Metaphors emerge, new perspectives appear,*
> *and new ideas and solutions surface*
> *as the brain gets stimulated in new ways.*

Because most of Expressive Arts is non-verbal, it encourages the individual to stay in body sensations and feelings rather than second-guessing and overriding the feelings with thinking, judging, or analyzing the experience.

Expressive Arts is different than traditional talk therapy in that it allows for process/goals to transpire in a non-verbal way. Sometimes language and words are not enough. Sometimes finding words is difficult. Young people in particular usually do not have the life experience, articulation, and understanding that are required to communicate their feelings and thoughts. Words in themselves can be limiting in the expression of feelings. Doing art allows those feelings to be expressed, witnessed, and acknowledged as they are being experienced by the maker.

Discoveries are made in the exploration, and perspectives are unique and meaningful to the maker.

The reader can work on an issue and focus on creative play and/or stress relief. The focus could be artistic, emotional, sensory, and/or aesthetic. The focus is totally dependent on the goal of the participant, the group, and the workshop.

My hope is that the methods given in this book will help in deepening your life, as it already has for so many others.

Introduction: Third Edition

Loving Your Life has been going strong for 12 years. After the first edition sold out, I refreshed *Loving Your Life* to reflect my intensive studies in expressive arts. The second edition was also well received, and after recent international travels with expressive arts I have refreshed it again. The core content remains the same, but now Loving Your Life is internationally compatible, sensitive to other cultures around the world.

I have intentionally kept the language simple and the format easy to read so that the goal of living life creatively and intuitively remains accessible to everyone, including readers whose first language is not English.

It is an honour to bring the book to you. Completing the creative practices offered here will help you love your life! Enjoy!

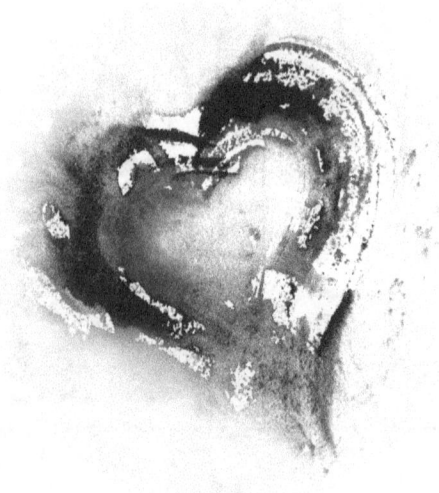

How to Use This Book

TRY, EXPERIMENT! Either take baby steps or put your seat belt on! RISK, get muddy, have fun, and try again. Be playful! It's okay if it feels a little scary.

Remember that your life is a journey that is uniquely yours. Consider this book as an offering of ideas; you decide what you want to read first.

Interspersed throughout the book are "creative practices" and personal reflections. The creative practices are skill-building exercises. The reflections are insights and observations that can help to inspire and motivate you—or perhaps just brighten your day.

What to expect while using the book

Sometimes learning a new skill is a struggle. The process of learning can be awkward. The newness and unfamiliarity may bring on anxiety. This anxiety could be fear of the unfamiliar or the familiar; fear of the unknown or fear of a perceived known; fear of failure or fear of success. Consider where your awkwardness is coming from. Perhaps similar body feelings have come up in previous sessions and there is unconscious anticipation of the same occurring here. Always honour yourself and listen to yourself. Be gentle and take your own time. If you get discouraged, try something else. With familiarity and experience come confidence.

Consider the support of a fellow reader and/or friend with whom to check in, exchange ideas and insights, and play.

Consider this book as something similar to a smorgasbord of food. Some days, you want to try everything; other days, you might crave desserts . . . or just meat and potatoes. Each day and each moment is unique. Only you will know what is right for that time. And if you are not sure what is right for that time, perhaps the creative practices and suggestions in this book will help.

How do you feel today? What are your choices? Know that your choices will change throughout your life journey, and that's all right. So how do you do this? How do you accomplish it? The idea sounds simple, but where do you begin? As you use this book, you might like to try documenting your thought processes and/or feelings in a small journal.

In this book, I share with you tools that have great value for me, my children, my students, and my clients. They are tools that I personally use and that I share in my workshops with great success and good response.

You may find that some tools are already part of your foundation. My hope is that you will continue building your resources.

Others may come easily to you. The unfamiliar tools just take more practice, like any new skill. From experience, I have found as we combine the tools, their effectiveness will increase exponentially. As we go from one art discipline to another, new perspectives arrive. The arts stimulate the brain in new ways of thinking.

> ***You are most knowledgeable about your life,***
> ***and the arts will put the pieces together***
> ***in a meaningful way for you.***

Know that we are all unique, with unique strengths and weaknesses. Support and consider your strengths and weaknesses with compassion. Try, risk, experiment, experience, and practise. Your weaknesses can be a source of strength because they are a place of great learning for you and can help to open up all the other creative possibilities within you.

chapter one

THE BEGINNING

Great changes in life are the result of gradual and cumulative effects.

THE BREATH OF LIFE

Everyone breathes.

In fact, you probably only become aware of your breathing when attention is called to it. But did you know that learning to breathe well is important for your physical, emotional, and mental health?

> **Deep breathing is a powerful relaxant as well as a rejuvenator.**

Breathing slowly lowers heart rate, metabolic rate, and blood pressure, and it eases muscle tension. Breathing deeply and slowly cleanses, refreshes, detoxifies, and energizes mind and body.

Becoming aware of your own breathing and taking time for deep-breathing exercises brings you in tune with your body and also provides energy and calm for deliberate and productive thinking. In slowing down / calming down, our intuition is clearer and stronger.

Children breathe naturally and deeply. Somehow we have unlearned that.

Today, notice how many times you hold your breath.

Each time you think of it, breathe deeply at least three times.

- Sit, stand, or, if possible, lie down. Keep your spine straight to get the feel of your belly's movement.
- Do not cross any limbs. Feel loose. Relax.
- Gently place your fingers—slightly interlaced and barely touching—on your abdomen, resting on your navel. As you inhale through your nose into the deepest part of your lungs, allow your stomach to expand as your fingers are pushed apart.
- Exhale slowly through your mouth, pushing out as much air as possible.
- Try this again.

Whatever you are doing, try to be aware of how you are breathing.

Enjoy your breathing!

Once this feels comfortable, try exhaling from the bottom of your spine, extracting all the air out of your system. Open your mouth in a relaxed fashion and notice how air naturally comes into your lungs. Exhale again. Be patient—it is a subtle sensation. The breathing becomes the action of exhaling only, and the air comes in naturally on its own to fill the empty lungs.

Breathing to breeze through your day

Proper breathing awareness can be incorporated into your daily life in many ways.

Whenever you think about breathing, straighten your back, drop your shoulders, and consciously breathe deeply a few times.

Imagine a string holding you by the top of your head attached to the sky.

Do this at your desk, in your car, walking, reading, on the phone, to start your day, to end your day, or even in anticipation of a stressful experience. Do it before a meal, to begin a meeting, before a test, or in class. Do it whenever you want to calm or refresh yourself.

Start by paying attention to the way you usually breathe. Is it quick and shallow? When practising deep breathing, slow down if you begin to feel light-headed. Your body might not be used to all the oxygen it's getting. Like anything new, breathing deeply takes practice and getting used to.

If deep breathing is new to you, practise it before you combine it with other exercises and activities. When you set aside time for breathing, do so before meals or at least two hours after a meal, use a well-ventilated room or go outdoors, and wear loose clothing. This will help you to get the most benefit from your deep breathing.

Try giving yourself gentle reminders to breathe deeply until it becomes a habit. You could try Post-it Notes on cupboards or mirrors, or inspirational posters or artwork that remind you to breathe deeply and slowly.

CREATIVE PRACTICE

Getting in touch with your breathing

The posture

- Sit relaxed, spine straight; shoulders back, down, and loose; with your hands on the arms of a chair or in your lap, not crossed; and your feet flat on the floor. Or, you can also stand, with feet shoulder-width apart and knees slightly bent. Or you can lie down, flat on your back.
- Place one hand on chest and one on upper abdomen, above your navel.
- Close your eyes to heighten awareness of how you breathe. Do you breathe into your chest or into your abdomen? Do you breathe quickly, slowly, or at a moderate rate? Do you breathe through your nose or through your mouth? Find your own rhythm—then slow it down, just a little bit each breath.

Try these steps:

- With eyes closed, breathe through your nose, feeling the air move down into your lungs as your chest and belly slowly rise and your shoulders straighten.
- Exhale slowly through your mouth and feel your abdomen and then your chest deflate and your shoulders relax.
- Continue breathing this way for ten more breaths.

Concentrate. See if you can notice the slight temperature change between cool air entering your nose and warmer breath leaving your mouth. Follow your breath and imagine that you are travelling with it through your nose, nostrils, and swirling down into your lungs, then slowly pushing back out through your mouth.

Right now, know that all you have to do is breathe, nothing else. If your mind starts to wander, as it will, gently bring your concentration back to focus on breathing. You may need to do this often, and that's all right. It may have been a while since you have slowed down enough to be aware of your breathing. This quieter sensation of slowing your body down may seem unfamiliar.

Finish with a cleansing breath.

- Breathe in deeply through your nose to a slow count of four, then hold your breath for another slow count of four.
- Exhale slowly through your mouth for a count of four.
- Push out the last bits of air through your mouth, making puffing sounds.

Try this cleansing breath at the end of your exercise. Do this at least three times. Exhaling through your mouth is a stronger detoxifying breath than exhaling through your nose. Note: You can also do this cleansing breath with the exhale method mentioned on page 3.

Sometimes, unfamiliar experiences feel uncomfortable at first—like writing with your non-dominant hand or sleeping on the other side of the bed. Discomfort sometimes shows up as tiredness, giggles, or boredom. But after you have tried these new things a few times, they become comfortable and familiar. Like any skill, breathing properly often takes practice. In the meantime, you benefit right away, building your overall health.

There are many forms of moving and breathing exercises and relaxation exercises; for example, yoga, tai chi, qigong, and mindful walking. Join a group and enjoy a new awareness of your breathing and your body.

Rejuvenating wake-up breathing

- Sit comfortably in a relaxed position.
- Inhale to a slow count of six.
- Hold for one count.
- Exhale for a slow count of three.

Find your own rhythm. Be sure to breathe in longer than out, thus feeding yourself oxygen.

Repeat until you feel wide awake.

Breathing to induce sleep and deep relaxation

- Lie or sit in a relaxed position.
- Inhale for three counts.
- Hold for one count.
- Exhale for six counts.

As you breathe out, permit yourself to become increasingly relaxed by releasing the tension slowly out of your body with the exhaling breath. Repeat until you are relaxed or asleep.

Breathing to get in touch with yourself

Just as breathing can relax and invigorate our bodies, so, too, can it relax and invigorate our minds. That's why the practice of meditation begins with awareness of our breathing.

Meditation can take many forms and serve many purposes. It can be performed as a momentary stress reliever, or a way of life.

In meditation:

- You bring your awareness to your mind and your thoughts, become aware of your mind, and rest there.
- You let go of worry, fears, distress, and pain. Clear your mind of any desire. As you let go of these tensions, your heart will sense confidence and a growing understanding.

Meditation can be described as a state of "being":

Being present	Understanding
Being aware	Watching
Being awake	Stopping a while to listen
Paying attention to life	

> **Meditation can help you be more thoughtful and more in control of your thoughts. Meditation can help relieve stress and is used for pain management. By getting to know yourself in meditation, you can become the master of your happiness.**

Often my students worry about meditating "correctly." They think their minds must be empty of thought. Because we have a mind, we're always going to have thoughts and emotions. A lot of the time, our minds run unleashed and wild. We can be easily distracted by what's around us or by chatter in our minds.

Sometimes when I begin to meditate it feels impossible to slow my mind down. However, the very action of trying to slow down or unwind is beneficial. Meditation does not eliminate thought, but instead helps us reflect and consider the thought by eliminating chatter. As our mind relaxes and our thoughts slow down, the spaces between thoughts become longer. Lengthening these gaps is the real work of meditation.

Meditation can take many forms. The following meditative breathing practice takes two forms—moving and sitting.

Moving breathing (qigong)

Why moving? In moving, I am more in my body and less in my head. Sometimes I need to move to slow down.

To help his warriors to increase their attention and focus, Marshall Yue Fei of the Song Dynasty used a series of moving breathing exercises. Follow the steps of this particular breathing exercise and enjoy the stretching of your arms and expansion of your lungs.

- Stand looking straight ahead, with your feet shoulder-width apart, your back straight in the pelvic tilt position, and your knees slightly bent. (To assume a pelvic tilt position, pretend you are about to sit. As you begin to sit, your pelvis will slightly rock forward, your buttocks will sink slightly and your balance will rest in the centre of your body.)

- Gently intertwine your fingers and bring your arms out in front of you as if you are hugging a barrel. Lower your arms, keeping them around the imaginary barrel. With your arms in this position, breathe in, still hugging the barrel while slowly raising your arms to shoulder height. As you exhale gently, lower your arms slowly back to your navel.

- Still in the hugging-the-barrel position, with fingers intertwined, breathe in and raise your arms above your head. Let your eyes follow your hands to the sky.

- On the exhale, gently separate your fingers and gradually bring your arms down in a wide arc. Follow this motion in your peripheral vision until your arms reach shoulder height. Looking ahead, continue to bring your arms down to your belly as you finish exhaling.

When you breathe in, concentrate on expanding your lungs as much as you can. When you breathe out, concentrate on contracting your belly.

Steps one to four constitute one set. Depending on instructors and styles, there are many variations. Take your time to work up to six sets of this exercise.

Sitting breathing

- Assume the posture we used when first getting in touch with our breathing: Sit relaxed; spine straight; shoulders back, down and loose; your hands on the arms of a chair or in your lap, not crossed; and your feet flat on the floor.
- Sit alone in silence. Balance your head, close your eyes, breathe in and out gently, and imagine yourself looking into your heart.
- As you slow your breathing down a little, slow your thoughts down a little.
- Be calm, focusing solely on breathing.
- Slow your breathing a little more—slow your thoughts a little more.
- If it's helpful, repeat a one-syllable word such as "love," or "peace," or another word that fulfills you. Or, if you like, count the breath. For example, "one" for the inhale, "two" for the exhale, "three" for the next inhale, and so on. Focus on that word while leaving all other thoughts behind. Slow the word down a little at a time. Now try to imagine the space before and after that word. Focus on the spaces. This takes practice and concentration. In time, the spaces will get longer. When you can achieve this calm space, you will connect with the truth of energy and the universe. At this level, it is said that you will find your highest thoughts, and your wisdom will come to you.

How long do I need to sit meditatively?

Entering a state of mindfulness is less about the length of time and more about the quality of time. Five minutes of wakeful practice is more valuable than twenty minutes of dozing.

Begin practising with short sessions. Inevitably, restless, busy thoughts will intrude. When this happens, gently bring yourself back to your focus. As you continue to practise, being in focus will come with greater ease.

Sometimes it may feel as if you cannot relax your mind or keep it focused. This is all right because being aware of your tense mind is part of being mindful. Stay present with your mind, and when your thoughts wander, gently bring them back to your focus. Allowing your breath to slow down will help your mind to slow down, too, a little bit at a time.

Returning to everyday life

As you re-enter everyday life, let the wisdom, calm, insight, humour, compassion, and spaciousness you gained in meditation filter into your day.
Be completely present in your actions.

The true miracle of practising meditation is ordinary and practical. It is a subtle transformation of your mind, body, and soul.

Inspire yourself to meditate with candles, incense, artwork that lifts your spirits, music that feeds your soul, dew on a flower petal, sunlight through the trees, a clear blue sky, and rich velvet. Try different approaches. Slowly, you will become master of your own bliss with a collection of remedies that will delight, inspire, illuminate, and elevate your every breath and moment.

Slowing the mind
is naturally peaceful and blissful

Just because you meditate, it doesn't necessarily mean you won't be running around, or that you will be calm all the time. It means that you'll be more aware and present because you stopped for a while to listen, to pause, to watch, and to understand.

THINKING ABOUT TIME

Time is everywhere, yet it eludes us.

Time haunts.

We try to manage our time, prioritizing, organizing, cleaning, setting goals, and defining purpose; yet time teases us as it keeps moving.

I am not asking you to reschedule your time but to think about it. Do in your life what is worthwhile; consider activities of value. Consider time and choices well spent and not time wasted.

Have you ever really thought about what it means to "take your time"?

"I'm too slow," moan some of my art students with a judgment of being "less than" and inadequate. When someone has worked quickly and easily to produce an interesting piece of work, the tendency is to negate the piece as of no value because it was not laboured over at that particular moment. In fact, some work ethics or belief systems disregard any talent or process done with ease. But the preamble to achieving such a piece or any work is often overlooked. Our strengths usually come with a sense of ease, enjoyment, and passion.

There can be such conflicts about time and value. In some situations, we are taught that "the time factor" equals "the dollar factor," which equals "the success factor." Speed and quantity seem to have great value in industry and business. Are you being harsh with yourself when measuring your value in dollars earned, or judging yourself in comparison with the achievements of others?

Often, in a group situation, if you are not keeping pace with the instruction, you feel slow and somehow inadequate.

For over thirty years as an instructor and painter, I have observed that we all work at different speeds for different tasks. Experience, tools, knowledge, confidence, headspace, physical capability, stress level, strengths, and time limitations are some of the factors that can affect our pace. Schedules, bells, and clocks are part of our lifestyle. Are time limits pressuring you?

Ponder this: in a day, most tasks are pressed into a specific time limit because yet another task awaits. The stress is in performing the current task while simultaneously planning the next. The experience is fragmented, unfocused, and not enjoyed.

Do all tasks have to be done by you today?

Is the time stress your responsibility?

How often do you consider taking extra time for at least some of the day's tasks? Becoming aware of time allotments and developing your own pace may require conscious effort and practice.

Taking your time: setting your own pace

When I began an intensive year of studying calligraphy with my instructor, American calligrapher Reggie Ezelle, he noted that if there was one thing he could teach us, it would be to slow down.

What happens when you slow down?

- Slowing down pulls you into the moment and into the experience by focusing your thoughts. When you hurry, you are looking ahead and working beyond the immediate task. In "hurry mode," you are not present. Hurried time flies, leaving a blur and little sense of pleasure.

- When you feel pushed, it's all right to tell others to stop pushing you. And it's okay to say that to yourself. We each work optimally at different tasks with varying speeds.

- In slowing down, you experience each aspect of the task and the process. When you take your time, you delight in what you are doing. In the awareness, you are alive and in the present moment. You have the opportunity to respond to the environment with heightened awareness of yourself and what you are reacting to.

- In slowing down, you recreate inner harmony, entering a place of peace where time stands still, the soul is fed, and you feel connected to all that is.

Take time to wander in detail;
get involved in whatever you are doing.
Take time to sharpen your awareness of each tiny detail;
feel your connection to your task and your relationship
to your surroundings.

Notice details and savour them.

How can you slow down?

There are many ways to slow down. Try different ways and discover which is most comfortable and works best for you today. It could be something else another day.

- What about a nap?
- Will you try tai chi?
- How about a walk in the woods or a nearby park?
- Why not give a friend a long hug? Notice his/her breathing.
- Can you step outdoors and still your rushing mind by breathing slowly for a while?
- Feel like hopping on a bike?
- Chanting?
- Mindfully watch yourself pour a cup of tea.
- Meditating?
- Watching the flame of a candle?
- How about a soothing bath?

You choose and you orchestrate. You are in charge of yourself.

When you feel your environment speeding up around you, and your chest tightening, make a deliberate effort to slow down and reclaim your peaceful inner landscapes.

Cancel some appointments and invitations. Quiet the chatter and the fury. Turn down the volume and turn down the throttle.

We all need to recover the spaciousness in our lives and to reconnect with the rhythms of nature. Sometimes less is more.

Sit in the dark. Calm all your senses.

Slowing down means discovering the time you already have —that priceless prize of time called life.

Take time to pause. That's another way of slowing down. It's in the pauses that life can also reveal itself.

Life gets an opportunity to catch up to us in those pauses. There is greatness in a pause.

A pause can create a calm waiting room for decisions. Deciding to wait can be your decision and your choice.

How often do you run past your goals, your dreams and opportunities?

Are you so busy whirling around stirring up dust that you can't see what the universe has for you?

It is in pauses that we can truly listen—especially to ourselves.

Practising patience is another way of slowing down.

Start by turning these pages slowly. Read slowly. Think about what you have read. Savour the moment. Savour your gifts.

Feeling safe

If it has been a while since you have truly slowed down, sat quiet, totally relaxed, the process may make you feel anxious, teary, or agitated. Other symptoms might show themselves as exhaustion, boredom, or giddiness. This is normal, as feelings and issues may come to the surface in the slowing-down process. Remind yourself that you are in control of your mind and body. Be gentle with yourself and soothe your breathing. Go as deep as you feel comfortable.

Resting

Now and then, give yourself permission to slow down and rest. Take a nap. Be totally unproductive for a while—perhaps even for one whole day. When I don't regularly slow down, I feel worn out, I make mistakes, I'm clumsy, I accomplish less, I am less patient and less satisfied.

> **Rest is not a luxury.**
> **It is a necessity for the healthy maintenance**
> **of your mind and body.**

For a moment, stop planning how you are going to accomplish a goal or use your talents.

Try to just be.

Enjoy being.

In my moments of slowing down, I have learned to see, to listen, to understand, and to grow.

As I learned to understand myself, I gained a deeper understanding and appreciation of my family and my world. I felt that I had become a part of creation again, instead of just bouncing around on the outside looking in.

- Take time to appreciate yourself, your family, and friends.
- Count your blessings.
- Count one blessing at a time . . . slowly, gratefully.

THE POWER OF THOUGHT

We have these choices: how and what we think;
how we respond; and what we choose to imagine.
Thoughts can affect situations and the people
around you. Each thought has energy of its own,
and it is thought that leads to action.

Prayer is one example of thought in action that can affect people profoundly. Humans are very sensitive to the energy of prayer, to the energy of a thought, whether negative or positive. Many of us can remember feeling the thoughts, warmth, love, and healing that have been sent our way. We sense support—or not. If we are aware, we often can sense the essence of a room, a situation, or a place. In turn, we can affect the room, the situation, and others with our thoughts.

Have you ever been so lost in thinking about someone that what you are doing seems suspended? Then, to your astonishment, the telephone rings, and it is the person you were thinking about? Sometimes, thoughts can be so strong that it is possible to hear sentences, see visions, and even feel the touch of another.

It is equally important to be able to filter thoughts that you do not want—such as dark or fearful thoughts.

Being committed to awareness and understanding
of your thoughts is important and powerful.
Like any skill, it takes time and practice.

More on managing and understanding thoughts and feelings will be discussed in chapter 3, page 67.

Thinking patterns

Berating ourselves

It is amazing how often we scold ourselves, while others may see a confident, tough, or funny individual. Few of us are confident no matter how secure we may appear, how blunt, tough, or funny we think we are. Deep inside, we are still sensitive, caring individuals.

> **Often we are too critical of our own behaviour,
> and if we aren't, then we may be
> allowing someone else to be.**

Worrying

Are you making a hobby of worrying? Worrying is thinking about things that have not happened yet. Worry does not change things. Worry is being afraid and could be considered *negative meditation*. Being afraid begets negativity. Consider the fear that causes you to worry. With careful reflection, transform your worrying into a constructive form of caring and action.

> **Worrying can be a habit that puts
> your thoughts into a dark hole.
> It will take determination to redirect them
> and fill your mind with more constructive thoughts.**

Being real

Look at the situation for what it is. This may sound simple, although many times I see how stress, anger, fear, worries of failure, habits, and past experiences distort how we look at a present situation.

> **The most powerful thinking is NOW thinking.
> Be in the moment.
> See what is in front of you.**

Manifesting our thoughts

Do you ever notice that when you purchase a new vehicle, suddenly there are lots of similar ones on the road? Women notice this phenomenon when they become pregnant. Suddenly there seem to be so many pregnant women around.

This is common. If our brains registered and acknowledged each detail that we come across in an ordinary day, they would become overloaded with information. Our brain readily connects with the familiar.

This is one of the reasons why positive thinking works.

By thinking positively, you are programming your brain to recognize positive opportunities that are around at all times.

We all live in one world, and we can either choose to see and experience the opportunities and the gifts or focus only on the misfortunes and misery. We can accept the cup as half empty or half full. It's the same cup, the same life.

To help you manifest your wishes, visualize what you want for your life. Then write it down. Go one step further and take a small action toward that goal. Now, instead of just wishing, you're on your way.

Our thoughts are like magnets. Positive thoughts attract, recognize, and evoke positive effects; they clump together to form positive happenings.

"Feel-good" attitudes also bring about more "feel-good" situations. This is why practising gratitude is so powerful. The more we practise being grateful the more we notice what we have to be grateful about.

One thought + faith + commitment
= manifestation of that thought.

More time invested in a thought equals more energy toward that thought. Timing, faith, and clear intent can take a thought to instantaneous manifestation.

CHOOSING YOUR STATE OF MIND

*You can choose how you think and what you think about.
You choose what you want to imagine.*

Work with the supportive ideas and creative practices throughout this book to guide your mind toward its highest potential. Your happiness depends on your state of mind and the choices you plan and carry out. We will talk more about strengthening your happiness in chapter eight.

Your state of mind includes your attitude, thinking patterns, and habits, as well as your emotions. Only you have control of how you think and what you choose to think about. You can rethink, retrain, and develop your thinking habits. You can expand joy in your mind, and that ripples out into your life.

Try and take some quiet time each day to reflect on how you feel and what you have been thinking about. During the day, in different situations, be aware of your thoughts. Are they reactive, angry, fearful, or insecure? Or are your thoughts pleasant, positive, and visionary? Some thoughts may surprise you when you take stock of them. Be nonjudgmental; just note them and acknowledge them for what they are.

As you become aware of the quality and direction of your thoughts, you will be able to evaluate their tone. This could be the time to reflect on the source of those thoughts. What inspires you? What bothers you? What can you do? What is the opportunity, here?

Are your thoughts busy, cluttered, confused, negative, scattered, or repetitive? Often we think the same thought over and over. That's when it is time to houseclean and organize thoughts. Just like anything else, your central thinking place needs regular cleaning and care to function. The exercises on slowing down and resting will result in awareness and retraining.

*You are the master of your brain.
Take charge.*

My studio used to be downstairs from my dwelling area. In my walk down the steps, my mind did not automatically enter the creative mode. So, on reaching the art studio, I often used breathing and music to transport my mind to my creative zone.

I begin my day with my own personal daily practice. This practice is a conscious effort to set a positive, grounded tone for the day.

All day, different activities keep me grounded, creative, and open to possibilities. If my daily practice isn't enough for what life brings me, I increase my self-care routine, perhaps by taking longer walks, by dancing, music, and/or humming. I work with whatever tools I seem to need that day to keep me calm and connected to the present. In chapter eight, more is discussed about daily practice.

Choices

You can choose what you put into your mind.

Like the rest of your body, what you put in comes out. Be selective in what you listen to, what you watch and read, what you do, and what you attend to. Seek out those persons in your life who have a positive manner and attitude. Imagine being free of endless commercials and just having music that fortifies your soul, and theatre and movies that build your mind and spirit. Choose positive feelings, positive speech, and positive actions.

Remind yourself that only you can select positive stimuli to enhance your precious life. And why would you do otherwise?

Make some choices today to add warmth and thoughtfulness to your life with music, tapes, CDs, language, and visual oases. While you cannot always make the choices you would prefer in your personal and professional world, you can definitely choose your attitudes, your responses, your actions, and your imaginings.

> ***Being aware and vigilant about***
> ***the choices we make gives us a sense of***
> ***purpose and empowerment.***

CREATIVE PRACTICE

Smiling meditation

I have used this simple meditation in high-stress times. It was so successful that it rubbed off onto the people around me.

The "Inner Smile" meditation comes from the sixth century B.C. Taoist tradition. These Eastern masters regarded emotions such as fear, worry, anger, and sadness as low-grade energy. As we know from experience, these emotions drain us, causing stress and uncertainty in our minds. The true smile, they believed, produces high energy or high vibration or high life condition, energizing and healing our internal organs and nervous system.

The concept of smiling into your own body is warm and loving. Memorize this exercise and share it with a friend. Let each process flow from one body area to another.

- Begin by closing your eyes. Feel your eyelids touch.
- Be aware of your lips and how they touch.
- Slow your breathing down.
- Recall someone or something that brings a genuine smile to your mind. Let the positive energy from this smile turn up the corners of your mouth, lift your cheeks, and crinkle up the corners of your eyes.
- Let the smile radiate into your eyes, and into each ear. Let the smile permeate your head.
- Imagine this smiley feeling in your mouth. Send the smile down your throat.
- Smile through your heart. Feel your heart smile.
- Smile into your lungs. Slowly let that smile ripple into your other organs.
- Smile into your back and muscles; smile into your bones.
- Feel the warmth of this smile radiate energy throughout your body and to any area that needs a little help today.
- Finish by smiling into your eyes again.
- Take a few moments to jot down any sensations and thoughts you had while doing this meditation.
- Maybe write a short poem . . .
- Begin each line with:
  A smile is . . .
  A smile is . . .

FREEING YOUR IMAGINATION

Imagination is an amazing tool. By unleashing your thoughts, letting them wander, sometimes to just daydream, you can conjure up anything. Your imagination is private and has no limits. You are the creator of these productions.

How can fantasy visions be useful?

Imagination can provide you with infinite choices.

It is here that you can explore, invent, and preview possibilities, scenarios, and prototypes of situations. By visualizing and analyzing, you can safely reflect and perhaps discover answers to your quests, your dreams, problems, and hopes.

There in your imagination, you can try "wild" if you are usually not; you can try "quiet" or you can try "freestyle." By occasionally just letting your mind wander freely, inspiration will reveal itself.

In your imagination, the impossible can happen, and it is there that solutions and ideas are free of any constraints. Formulate your dreams, fearlessly follow your desires, and take your time to explore whatever you want to experience. Be impulsive. Fantasize without boundaries.

Your imagination can give you revenge, fame, satisfaction, and more.

Your imagination can give you new perspectives.

Your imagination can give you hope.

Your mind is a canvas ready for any medium, special effects, fantasy, or state of mind.

By allowing a free flow of imagination without judgment, any possibility can present itself. Discriminating too soon could thwart the creative genius that we all possess.

Sometimes, let the scenes play out. Something imagined does not need to be acted upon. Other times, you may just need to do some mind housecleaning to reveal the creative essence under the rubble.

Imagination can help you to recall particular memories of vision, taste, feeling, sound, and smell. Such imagery can evoke physical and mental responses. For example, a particular smell could evoke a memory, then a response, and so on. Imagery can enhance your learning and accomplishments by fine-tuning your awareness.

Many forms of prayer and meditation use imagery as a tool to focus and to gather energy. Prayer and meditation are the first steps to put thought into action.

I use imagery in the breathing sessions that I introduce my art and creativity workshop with. My students inevitably discuss how this helps them to experience heightened learning and higher successes throughout the class and the rest of the day.

Getting results

If you are not getting the results in life that you want, then perhaps it is time to change your tack.

> *Everything*
> *you need and want is*
> *within you and around you.*

What changes could you make in your thinking, or in your way of doing things, to get the results you want?

If you think you have run out of possibilities, be still. Just imagine. It will come.

Learning to free your imagination and to use it as a tool for thinking and planning will also help you to increase your awareness of your own life and all that is around you.

YOUR SPIRITUAL SELF

Awareness of your spiritual self begins with curiosity—the sense that there is something more and greater than just yourself. Like a flower, which begins with a seed and unfolds into beauty, curiosity flowers into an intensity of awareness followed by wonder and profound appreciation.

Continued and deepening reflection intensifies all these stages and is accompanied by a growing sense of "mindfulness"—increasing perceptive awareness of detail in everything we do and see and feel.

Developing spiritual awareness connects each of us to energy within ourselves and beyond ourselves. Spirituality is connected to meditation and being mindful.

Nurture, inspire, and revitalize your spiritual self with mindful reading, participating in caring projects for others, stimulating your mind with uplifting song and music, and with quiet meditation. Your spiritual body gets hungry, too, just as does your physical body.

What is it to be "mindful"? One way to describe "mindfulness" is retaining an alert state of mind, with a heightened sensitivity to each detail. It is a way of being present. In being alert, you are acutely aware of:

- Yourself on many levels—your reactions, responses, thought patterns, physical body, morals, and so on
- Your surroundings—other people, home, your community, and nature
- A heightening of all your senses

Each spiritual path is deeply personal.

It is important to listen to your heart. Follow your heart.

Your life is worth it.

To be spiritual is to be aware.
As we are acutely aware,
we connect with something outside of,
and greater than, ourselves.

DEFINING YOUR PURPOSE

Having a purpose makes life worthwhile.

Setting goals and priorities that reflect our purpose keeps us focused on our purpose. I personally find that this makes it easier to follow my heart when making decisions. My purpose keeps my head clear and focused.

As you clarify your purpose in life, there will be a growing conscious sense of self. Actions and choices will become more deliberate.

Setting goals and expressing wishes helps them to come true. You can intuitively create circumstance and act on opportunities that will bring you closer to those goals.

Setting priorities generally keeps me happier and lowers my stress level. This is true whether I am prioritizing my life, my family, or just today's to-do list. Priorities can also pull us in opposite directions. There can be consequences, family obligations, cultural expectations, and so on. Priorities involving others requires balancing, compromises, boundaries, timing, and consultations.

No matter how we strive to be aware and focused, daily life still happens in ways that defy plans or goals. If we each accept our path and remain continuously open to seeing possibilities and obstacles as opportunities, then they can be readily turned into probabilities.

Always listen to your heart. It is your passion.

When you have a big load, take time to quietly reflect and consider your options. I have experienced this time and time again: When I have a plan, I end up with time to spare. When I take quiet time and plan, life usually flows neatly into place. Not taking that planning time, especially when I think I cannot spare a minute, means that everything seems to take longer, my stress increases, and often the end result is not as successful.

When life feels misaligned and chaotic, it is a signal to pause, slow down, and reflect.

Prioritizing is critical. Especially when the best-laid plans are thrown into a loop by life.

How do the daily chores suddenly overrun you with stress? Are you doing too much? Are you doing the easy tasks first? Are you leaving the tough, longer jobs for last? These are ingredients for unnecessary and avoidable extra stress.

We all know that planning and prioritizing each day eases the strain of time deadlines and provides a sense of satisfaction. Let's do it! Write a list. Decide what is most important for the moment and do it first. Mark it off with a huge check mark, and the rest will follow.

Honest.

My Prayer

Help me
accept the miracle of my body, mind and spirit,
to open myself to endless possibilities,
to encourage goodness to permeate me,
and to radiate from me.

Help me welcome
my obstacles,
for they are the true friends
of growth and resource.
Help me be unafraid and
remember that I really am
good enough.

Help me realize that I am becoming
who I am my whole life long.
and I am born to play, carefree abandon all my right.

Help me remember that I am well taken care of
and that I can take care of myself.
Please remind me that we are all connected
and that my thoughts and actions affect all
that surrounds me.

Remind me to share my gifts.

And most of all, help me remain
grateful for the gift that is my life.
Thank you,   thank you,
thank you.

chapter two

CLEAR HEARING

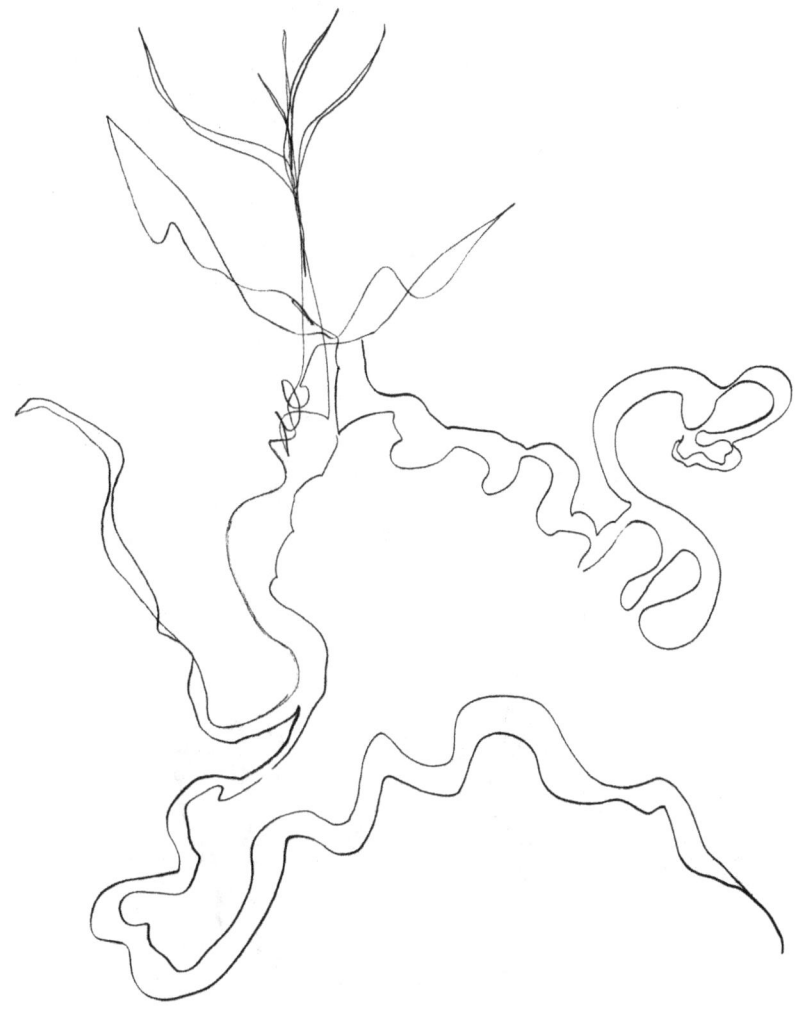

I need to hear myself.

I need to listen to myself.

When we don't know who we are
it is easy to compromise ourselves.

INTUITIVE LISTENING

One of my teachers, Ed Hagedorn, said that our intuition is correct 95 percent of the time. Those are pretty good odds. So how do I tap into my intuition?

> **Connecting with stillness by listening to myself fully has meant hearing my inner voice and taking the time to reflect on what I am hearing.**

To do this, I found it was necessary to slow down enough to really listen. It also meant valuing myself enough to act upon the messages I was becoming aware of.

Valuing myself also involved the willingness to change plans, to voice my needs, to follow my heart, and to do all this without judgment. Learning to trust my intuition, my body, my needs, and desires, came only gradually as I enhanced this ability to quiet other sounds and to listen to myself.

For so long, I felt that I was not being heard. This depressed, frustrated, and drained me. I thought I needed others to have the listening skills that I wanted. My reactions were directed outside myself. Curiously, when I finally did learn to listen to myself, I realized that I didn't need to project my needs on others.

> **First, I need to listen to myself and to be comfortable with myself.**

When I need an empathetic someone to hear my story, I have learned I can find that person. As my needs were being met, I found that I could articulate situations more clearly. Now the urgency to be heard outside myself is gone. I have found new patience within myself. I can listen to myself.

Occasionally, I fall out of my calm state when I am anxious, angry, frustrated, and fearful; these feelings block me from hearing my inner, intuitive voice. I am now able to notice how something has blocked my listening ability and I try to alleviate the source of my distress. It seems that I am constantly balancing myself. However, with time, effort, and practice, I have been able to shorten the distress and lengthen the calm, happy times.

Practising to listen

Listening well can become habitual.

As we practise to listen well to others, we practise to listen well to our inner selves. Each way of listening (to others and to ourselves) heightens our listening ability. By appreciating the act of careful listening, you will also realize the benefits of communication with others.

In my struggle to listen to myself, I became aware of hearing others more clearly than ever.

Are we offenders in the simple act of listening?

Too often, we react quickly with our own reactions and conclusions. We interrupt and interject with our own thoughts. Are we afraid to hear something from others? Or afraid we will lose our thought?

By your example of listening well, you also teach others that communication is important.

Poor listening could simply be a bad habit.

When you really listen, you are quietly intent on the speaker. You try to understand without judging, and you do not question or interrupt, even when you don't agree.

Empathic listening is when you allow the speaker to talk through troubles or ideas. You give her the space and time to process her ideas or problems, and to do so in her own way.

Holding back your own experience and "good" advice means truly respecting the other's intelligence and worth, as well as her life journey.

Trusting the process of listening also places trust in the discoveries of others, knowing that you will probably be learning something, too.

Acknowledge the truth of the statement spoken.

Sometimes the intensity of careful listening can tire you. Accept the other's gift of gratitude by knowing that you helped by simply listening.

Thinking before speaking

Before you speak, think about what you want to say. When you talk, speak slowly and try to use fewer words. Or don't talk at all. Communication is measured in more than just words.

- Just listen.
- Don't think about what you'll say next while someone else is talking.
- Thoughts will flow naturally into your head when it's your turn.
- Take time to respond. If action is necessary, it will be more fruitful after you have pondered.

What is careful listening?

When listening is really working, new doors open.

Thoughts, plans, and ideas flow more freely and clearly. Feelings are felt more deeply. Emotions are more intense. Your eyes may well up, your laughter may be brighter, and what began in anger may end in mutual understanding.

Your whole being will acknowledge your respectful attentiveness and will then move forward confidently to other experiences.

Careful listening helps us to open ourselves to ourselves as well as to others.

Blocks to listening

When we are not calm inside ourselves, it is impossible to hear our inner voice—or anyone else's voice—clearly.

When our brain chatter is busy, loud, angry, fearful, or reactive, we block ourselves from picking up subtle messages from others.

When your own needs are not being heard, it impairs your ability to listen to your intuition and to your world.

Whose reality?

> **We all have our own truth and our own perspective of what our reality is.**

As children, how many times have we said, "I'm thirsty," only to be told, "No, you're not." Simple, yet a harmful, negating answer.

The child acknowledges thirst in the body and, instead of acknowledging the body sense felt by the child, the adult negates it by saying, "No, you're not," instead of "I hear that you're thirsty; I'm busy. I'll get you a drink in a moment." The examples go on: "Stop crying," "Oh, this won't hurt," "Don't be silly," "Don't be afraid." Feelings are being negated.

The child is learning to recognize body needs and emotions and to express them. When adults negate such recognitions, confusion sets in, intuition is doubted, feelings are denied and suppressed. Emotional unhealthiness, defensive habits, and discord inhibit the mind and body, clouding creativity and the true self.

> *No one has the right to assume or to tell us what we are feeling.*

Each experience is unique and real to each of us. Situations are felt in a personal way. Each truth is real to us at the time. When we begin to accept those truths in each other, we then have a foundation to effectively communicate.

Active listening with language

> *Active or experiential listening is a supportive and non-interfering way of stating back to the speaker what he or she is communicating to you.*

This enables the speaker to hear what the listener heard. The speaker's message might not be quite what the listener heard.

Language has limitations in meaning and interpretation. What is said is relative to the individual's experience and culture. We hear and speak through the lens of our experience. It is important to note this. Framing and introducing ideas set up open communication and curiosity on both sides.

With words and impressions aired on both sides, wrong impressions can be corrected, and ideas fleshed out in detail, with a good chance of mutual understanding. Active listening helps people articulate their inner thoughts and processes and explore ideas and issues. Active listening also gives the speaker an opportunity to hear and understand himself when his thoughts are spoken back to him.

With active listening, repetitive thoughts and beliefs can be lifted out of limbo and brought toward clarity and understanding. We can then use experience and memory to transcend our old ways and contribute fresh thoughts and ideas.

How does active listening work?

Sometimes one speaker might want to talk through an entire issue before hearing a response from the listener; or the speaker might want to deal with one thought at a time. It helps to agree on a time limit for the exercise beforehand, and then place an unobtrusive clock nearby. From my experience, it is fascinating how I can intuitively regulate my attention without feeling that time is a restraint. Usually, the exercise is completed within five minutes of the pre-set time.

For the listener, active participation is more than a repetition of words. It involves communicating back to the speaker the thoughts, expressions, tone, and even the body language that has been related.

With practice, what at first may seem awkward and laborious can become a natural way of communication.

> *It is amazing how clear and uncluttered understanding becomes with the effort to listen intently.*
> *The energy saved on guesses and assumptions is liberating on both sides.*

Listening to your body

> *Body focusing is a way of listening to your body.*
> *Appreciate that your body remembers everything, is programmed for survival, and is constantly attempting to communicate to you what it requires.*

When you have a feeling—uneasy or pleasant—about a place, a person, or even an idea, pay attention to the feeling and check it out. Ask yourself how this feeling is coming about. Listen objectively to your inner voice.

When you feel uncharacteristically tired or out of sorts, pay attention to the feeling and slow down. Again, listen to what your inner voice has to say.

Ignoring these body sensations or pushing them away does not make them go away. These sensations get stuffed somewhere in the body and reappear by surprise when we are triggered in some way and are least expecting a reaction. This is a setup for dis-ease and discomfort.

It's healthier to accept and confront bodily sensations. We need to acknowledge them, experience them, and deal with them if we can.

When something is worrying you, when you feel hurt or angry, take some quiet time to sort out what is really bothering you. Talk to yourself or try to journal; and when that is not enough, talk with a good friend or someone close. Expressing yourself through painting, poetry, and/or music helps bring the feeling outside of yourself. Release the discomfort. Try to sense the source of your feelings. For example, your sickly stomach could indicate a warning, nervousness, anxiety, or fear. A cold could indicate that you are rundown and need rest. Headaches could indicate eye strain, tension, stress, worry, or uneasiness. Certain pains are alert signals. Get to know and trust your body. Note if any trouble seems to last. If you can't put a finger on the source, check it out with your health practitioner.

Listening to your inner voice

Listening to your body by attending to your feelings and energy has many facets.

> ***Becoming sensitive to listening to your inner voice,
> you will begin to listen to the many layers
> of possibilities, memories, experiences, habits,
> and fears that can influence that inner voice.***

Suppression can become habit, so instead of listening to yourself, you might be seeking "the answer" outside of yourself.

Ask yourself, "Where are these feelings coming from?" "What options are open to me?" "Is this the best answer for me?" "My life? My family? Community?" When contemplating our lives and choices, such reflective questions can help us to change old patterns and dramas that replay in our lives.

Ask yourself if that inner answer is based on fear or denial, or is truly in your best interest. Sometimes there is more than one level to an answer. Listen to them all and put them in their place.

What would your answer be, coming from a love centre?

What would your answer be, coming from a fear centre?

Try journalling or discussing that "inner voice" with a supportive friend.

Be still to really listen.

Communicating with your body

Body feelings can be expressed as sensations, images, or visions, as well as emotions.

Your feelings are an accurate indicator of balance and rightness in your life.

When something is unbalanced, your body knows it and immediately sets out to balance, repair, and heal itself. Your body is constantly checking in and adjusting itself to maintain this equilibrium.

We trust our body to maintain our temperature. If it is slightly out of line, we do not feel well and sense something is not right. As babies and children, we were very much in tune with our bodies. We made our demands known without inhibition, as every parent knows. As we grew older, judgment, pressure, criticism, intimidation, and negation may have taught us to discredit those feelings or to judge them as wrong or unimportant, and thus disregard or submerge them.

Feelings have many facets. Permit yourself to acknowledge your feelings and to stay with them for a while. Feelings serve some purpose, lesson, message, or strength.

By suppressing or denying those feelings—whether pleasant or unpleasant—they can become hostage in your body and in your mind. As time progresses, suppressed feelings can find expression in confused emotions. Over time, muddled feelings and misunderstood emotions can severely impact our ability to live a healthy, balanced life.

By consciously striving to develop an awareness of how you really feel about something, and taking time to think about it, such feelings will clarify or dissipate.

Expressing your feelings freely by participating in the arts, music, drama, movement, visual arts, and creative writing can help to discharge feelings safely and non-verbally, making way for clearer thinking and calmer emotions.

CREATIVE PRACTICE

Listening to your body

Find a quiet spot or time.

- Feel the different sounds that resonate in different parts of your body.
- Experiment by singing different vowels. Try humming the vowels.
- Notice your body as you sing. Notice your body before and after you sing. Can you notice any changes in your body?
- Listen to how various vowels resonate differently inside you. You may notice a certain vibration in your head, contrasted with how it feels inside your mouth, top of your cheeks, perhaps in various areas in your throat, chest, abdomen, and so on.
- Listening well gives you more energy, a happier disposition and improved vocal control.
- Sit quietly and look inward. Sit still, slow your thoughts and calm your mind. Relax your body. Make the effort to learn to listen again.
- Listen again. Stay with your body. Even if you begin with three minutes, listen regularly. Gradually build up the time you spend intentionally listening.
- Stillness guides us towards learning how to listen.

Generally in our society we are taught to search outside ourselves for knowledge and inner wisdom.

You have everything inside yourself. Pause, slow down, listen, and allow your inner wisdom to surface.

JOURNAL WRITING — HEALING WORDS

Writing is known as one of the cleansing and healing tools of the mind.

Writing utilizes the mind's tools of language and images to express thoughts and feelings, either factually or imaginatively.

Writing often provides the raw material for creating art. As with other art forms, such as songwriting, painting, and poetry, we often belittle our own ability to create. We often carry strong judgments on how art in any form should be expressed. We think that we aren't smart enough, original enough, or travelled enough.

Journal writing can be your private and unique act of expression without concern for form, style, grammar, or even punctuation.

Sometimes our thoughts are buried behind judgments, low self-esteem, personal doubt, and/or concern about the opinions of others. Journal writing is private and personal, and it's intended only for you. The act of writing random thoughts and describing ideas and images can release us from tension and put us on the threshold of exciting creativity.

Journalling can be wondrous.

Thoughts have a tendency to mill around in our minds. It often seems that the mind, when cluttered with unacknowledged thoughts, has little space to play with new ideas and creative possibilities. However, when writing down your thoughts, something transcendental happens. The act of writing them down seems to acknowledge their existence and permits you to move on. This creates more room for fresh thought and new ideas. These written-down thoughts become "something" outside yourself. One can look at these thoughts outside oneself, consider them, and turn the page.

Make room at the beginning of your day to sit for a few minutes and become quietly aware of your thoughts. Notice them throughout the day. You may soon become aware of how many thoughts keep repeating. By writing them down as they spin through your mind, they will slow as if being acknowledged and put on the shelf, leaving space for the next thoughts. As you check in with yourself, you will be learning about yourself.

Regular journal entries are another way to houseclean your thoughts. When you keep your house in order, clutter doesn't get out of hand. Regular journalling helps houseclean your mind, keeping it fresh, clear, and open for creative thoughts. It also provides a record of past ideas and concerns.

Another benefit from regular journalling makes one aware of language and words used.

Give it a try now.

CREATIVE PRACTICE

Journalling –
emptying the clutter from your mind

From time to time, it is important to empty your mind from all those words tumbling about that may be giving you a headache or holding back an avalanche of creative possibilities.

This exercise will help you to loosen up your mind and relax the usual meticulousness of your thoughts and judgments. This practice is a warm-up to help clean out the brain's cobwebs and perhaps uncover a gem of a thought, or release an avalanche of creative possibilities.

Using a pad of paper, a scribbler, a loose-leaf binder, or a blank bound book, just write whatever comes to mind. Be relaxed. Have fun. This creative practice is only for your eyes.

Pretend that you are the recording secretary for your thoughts. Edit nothing. Write whatever comes to mind, even if it is incomplete, even if your brain is rebelling, or you are thinking that you are stuck. Record it all. I tell my students it's all right to record a shopping list if that is what comes to mind, or even to write "I feel awkward." As you write down those seemly idle words as they come to mind—no matter what they are—new words and thoughts will replace them.

- Use a timer so that you are not preoccupied with looking at the time. Set it for ten minutes. As you become accustomed to journalling, write for as long as you need to.

There is no pressure here to produce a product.

This is just for you.

For journalling ideas see pages: 45, 202, 203, 222, 223, 236.

CREATIVE PRACTICE

27 Journaling Ideas

Your journal is personal, private and confidential. Perhaps it is a daily check-in? Perhaps a dumping ground? Perhaps it holds memories or gratitude? Maybe sketches? And/or a workbook for poetry?

Don't criticize your writing or your drawing. Do what feels right for you. Trust yourself to know what you need and follow your own impulses. Enjoy your road to discovery.

Here are some ideas that might be helpful to get started:

1. My hopes and dreams are…
2. In the future I want…
3. I wonder about…
4. What puzzles me is…
5. I am unsure about…
6. What's interesting is…
7. What's hard about this is…
8. One place I will grow is…
9. A strength for me is…
10. Something I am noticing is…
11. I'm surprised at…
12. I learned…
13. I am concerned that…
14. This is different because…
15. I feel connected…
16. It made me think about…
17. I could visualize…
18. I figured out…
19. I can relate this to…
20. How do I feel about myself today?
21. Did I comfort myself in any way?
22. Did I punish myself in any way?
23. How did other people treat me today, and how did I respond?
24. Was I more concerned about pleasing others than meeting my own needs?
25. Did anyone say something that sticks in my mind — that seems to have special meaning or importance for me?
26. Did I observe anything or do anything that left an impression on me?
27. When do I notice my body energy rising? And when do I notice my body energy dropping?

SOUND AWARENESS

In ancient cultures, sound was known as the Beginning.

Awareness of the importance of sound in your life may be an important beginning for you.

How can we appreciate sound if we don't listen?

How can we listen if we don't appreciate sound?

There is so much sound and vibration in our lives. Noise from computers, heaters, lights, motors, fans, air conditioners, filters, radios, generators, dryers, machinery, traffic, and more are constantly battering us.

When we learn to tune out some of the noise, we may also be tuning out sounds that could be important. How do we select and how do we edit? Do some sounds get filed in the "ignore" pile and others not? What messages need to be heard? Perhaps we don't even know. Who knows what we are missing?

As we block noise, are we also learning to block other senses and other sensations? Are we numbing ourselves to the world around us? No wonder that we're exhausted at the end of the day. We crave greenery and rivers and quiet.

Check out your environment throughout your day. Can some sounds be turned down? Can sound-emitting machines be moved or muffled? Can your work area be shifted to a quieter location? What can we control?

Try to take breaks from the cacophony of daily noise.

Turn off the TV. Turn down the radio. Find a quiet area to read or just to reflect. Spend time in a visual or aural sanctuary like a forest, a garden, or a park. If that's not possible, develop images in your mind of quiet, restful spaces, and now and then tune out from the noise and just visualize those places. Think of the silence of underwater scuba diving, the gentle slapping of water against a canoe. Imagine yourself in a comfy wicker chair on a sunny porch. If outside noise is preventing this, use headphones and nature tapes until you can do this in a natural environment.

Sometimes, turn everything off and just sit quietly.

Pull up those calm, silent visions.

Listen to the sound of silence and feel yourself relaxing.

MUSIC

Music is associated with creation.

The ancient world knew the miraculous power of music for harmonizing body and spirit.

Many cultures still use various sounds to inspire healing, for spiritual enlightenment, and for tuning into the energy of the universe.

Music is a universal language, and anyone can benefit from its uplifting powers. It has no barriers of prejudice or location.

Musical vibrations can stimulate everything. If it is true that plants grow best near calming music, then surely calming music is good for humans, too.

- Select music to enhance your life.
- Listen and note how various kinds of music make you feel.
- Which style relaxes you?
- If you want to rev up, what type of music does that for you?

I use music in my workshops as background or sometimes as a focusing tool. Participants comment on their relaxation level and their successes. Observers notice increased calm and concentration in the students. The few times when I have left music out, my students tell me they miss it.

For workshops, I try to pick music that blends into the background. Music can relax and mellow a classroom or liven it up.

Music can evoke powerful emotions and unlock either happy or traumatic experiences stored in our memory. Combining music with imagery and other art forms intensifies and expands the experience.

CREATIVE PRACTICE

Seeing shapes in sounds: experimenting with sound's rhythms, shapes, and colours

Gaining a deeper awareness of sounds can help you to understand how sound affects you. Explore different ways of experiencing sound. Use colours, shapes, and journalling to give expression to the sounds you hear.

Consider different musical instruments, like a drum, shakers, violin, piano, flute, and so on, and try to understand how each affects you. Are the sounds soothing, irritating, inspiring, heartfelt, sad . . .

Also collect musical recordings using instruments in different ways and from different cultures. For example, for drumming, try East Indian, African, North American Indian, Chilean, and jazz kit drumming. Option: listen and explore your response to sounds of daily living; for example, a blender, a ringing phone, a boiling kettle, or water dripping.

Practice one

- With your eyes closed, breathe deeply for a few minutes, and then listen attentively to one of the selected sound pieces.
- Let the shapes of the sounds drift into your mind.
- With a pencil and paper, mark down the general line and/or shape that the particular sound piece is prompting for you. For example, a low note may appear large and round, and a high note may appear tight and small. Do the shapes feel connected or separate? When you are ready, continue with another piece.

Different rhythms in sounds may reflect your rhythm of transcribing; for example, for a fast beat, short, quick strokes. The sounds from different musical instruments will prompt various shapes and reactions.

Practice two

- With a selection of crayons or markers in front of you, listen to a sound selection.
- Breathe deeply and close your eyes. Open yourself to letting the music stimulate colour in your imagination.

- Record the shapes in colour as you listen to each musical piece. For example, a high note may appear bright for you.
- To deepen your sound awareness and experience further, on a separate piece of paper describe the shapes and colours you just made. Use descriptors such as, "jagged, sharp line"; or "round, thick lines"; or "tiny, spiralling red lines," and so on. After you have done so, answer these questions: What did it feel like to paint from start to finish? Any distractions? What about the movement of the lines? Quick or slow?

I have shared this creative practice with different groups. We have numbered the pieces as we go along. In our sharing, it is fascinating to see that each musical piece had a character and feeling that we could collectively feel, along with our individual interpretations.

Practice three

This exercise takes the previous exercise a step further.

- Listen to musical selections as suggested previously.
- Write down or describe the thoughts, words, phrases, ideas, or memories that come to mind. Do not judge the process or order of your words. Just record them.
- Any surprises? Have you discovered anything new?
- Write as long as you wish.
- How can you use these discoveries in your life?

The process of journalling accomplishes at least two important goals. It provides a reflective pause in your activity and increasingly helps you to express yourself. Sometimes I am surprised by what I journal. I have recalled buried memories and recounted glorious experiences. I have learned new things about myself. Sometimes I organize the day or the rest of my life. Other times, the journalling is just a way to clear my mind.

Rhythm and vibration

Exploring different rhythms is something that we feel with our whole body. When the music is right for us, we want to yield to it and move with its rhythms and vibrations. We feel motivated, relaxed, and rejuvenated.

Scientifically speaking, we are energy vibrating at a cellular level. All other matter is vibrating, too. Since vibrations are rhythms, everything is rhythm. All vibrations interconnect and interact with each other.

Life is challenging enough without going against the natural rhythms of the world around us.

In nature, it takes less energy to pulse together than to pulse in opposition, so similar rhythms tend to align over time. Becoming aware of the signals within our bodies helps us align with and communicate with other rhythms. As you explore rhythm, you tap into collective energy. It is indescribable. Experiencing it is the only way.

Body rhythms and patterns

We are all musical. We are born with body rhythms and patterns. Our bodies are rhythm machines, in and out of sync, creating patterns and chaos. Our heartbeat is the most familiar. In native traditions, it is said that, when we drum, we are echoing our heartbeat for the earth.

Listen.

Listen more.

Respond.

When exploring different rhythms, relax and let your whole being feel and move to the vibrations. You will know in your body and in your mind and with all your senses the rightness of what rhythms resonate with your rhythm. You will feel it in your hands and in your feet, and you will want to give in to the rhythm. Dare to let yourself go.

Dance with passion

Dance ugliness, dance anger, and dance wildly. Sweat. Even if you hate the music, give in to it! Dance as if you hate it! Respond to it!

Dance fearful!

Dance is about passion. Dance dreamily, softly, gracefully, and exotically.

Dance anywhere. Dance with life as your lover.

Dance gleeful! For no other reason except for glee itself, jump! Do a cool move! Do an awkward move. Tell a story in your dance.

The body needs to move and to dance. Sing and hum to your own rhythm and timing.

Drumming, dancing, chanting, singing, and humming are ways to infiltrate other vibrations into your cells. As you practise awareness of your rhythm, you will be able to further relate to other rhythms around you. These rhythms of humanity, of the weather, earth cycles, society, and systems are everywhere. With your regained sensitivity, you will be able to adjust yourself and resonate with similar rhythms, thus gaining some harmony with your surroundings.

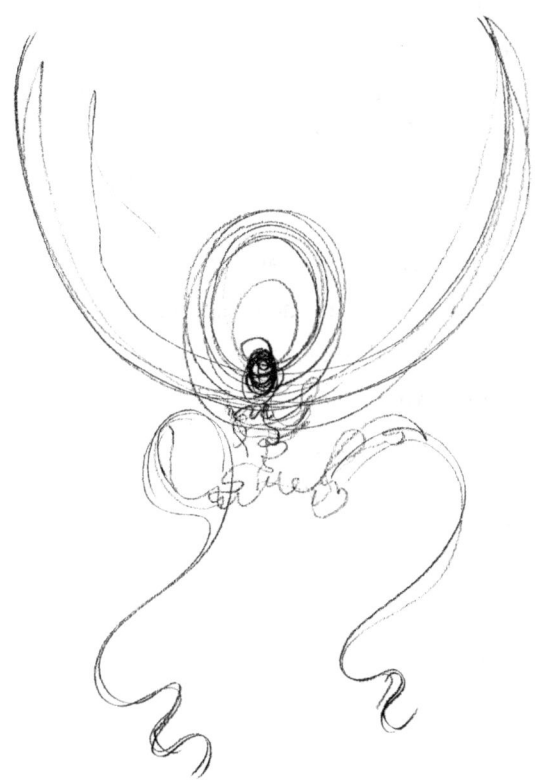

CREATIVE PRACTICE

Giving yourself to music

In dance, I can give myself to the rhythm of the music. I don't have to think or solve anything. My body can just physically be. Tap your toe, rock your head, sway, move any way you like. That's all. That's enough.

Initially, try experiencing the music in a space with no mirrors, so you do not feel any judgment on how you move, or if you move, or even how you look. Try this experience on your own or with a supportive group where it is safe to move without judgments or expectations.

Let yourself become one with the music. Imagine that you are swallowing the music and take it in deeply.

Try a song that you connect to.

Try slow, soft songs, happy lyrical songs, hard, heavy songs, erratic, chaotic songs, and easy, smooth songs.

Sense your body. What are you feeling? How is your body responding?

What areas react first?

What parts of your body resist movement?

Try moving as if you are performing on a stage.

Try moving as if you are with a lover.

Move as if you are in water.

Remain acutely aware of your movements.

Feel the energy of the music so you are not separate anymore. Become one with the music.

Did you sweat?

Did you have fun?

Did you giggle or cry?

And sometimes, while you are dancing, add your voice. Sing out loud! Yell! Moan! Sigh . . .

At the beginning, your voice might feel tight or shy. You have a wide range of tones and volume. Use it all to express how you feel.

Notice how your voice can create different vibrations in your body.

Hum.

Hum with the music and feel the vibrations of the humming inside yourself.

Hum throughout the day

Then, note how you feel.

How would you draw your dance?

How would you paint your dance?

Be still . . .

What is happening in your body?

chapter three

CHALLENGE AND CHANGE

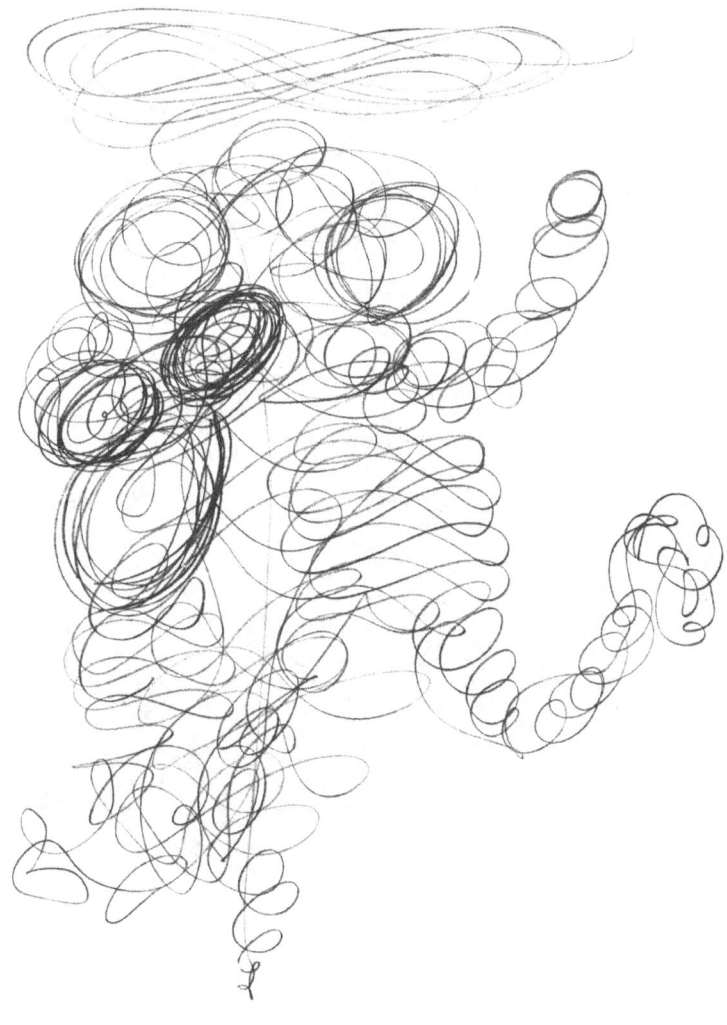

When you are clearer you
make better choices.

And good choices can enrich your life.

ABOUT CHANGE

*The difficulty of making changes—any change—
resides in our ego and our fear of the unknown.*

Sudden, harsh, and/or traumatic change upsets our existence, including those around us. All change is loss.

Fast change or too much change often creates stress and/or panic because it challenges our routine comfort and stability. Slow change can sometimes leave us restless or impatient. Are we ever satisfied with how change transpires?

Familiarity is comfortable to a degree, even though we may not like all that it entails. At least it is predictable. Change, even if secretly desired, represents the unknown. We fear the unknown to a greater or lesser degree, whether we admit it or not. That is because change disrupts familiar patterns and beliefs.

In a situation where a job ended, a contract was cancelled, or a relationship fizzled, perhaps we initially felt distraught. Yet possibly, shortly after, we felt relief and secretly even felt glad, because that particular situation was not good for us anymore.

Do you often ignore that inner voice urging you to change in some way? Is it because carrying on is easier, even when the situation may not be a good one? Would change entail giving up something or offending someone, or making an effort? Do you often console yourself with the status quo by considering that the change might not work out after all, so why bother?

What opportunity is in the change?

Do these self-conversations sound familiar?

The challenge of change

How do you cope with change?

What do you do when change happens quickly?

What is it about change that you don't like?

Suppose it's not fun or it is traumatic? Do you scream, complain, sulk, cry, get drunk, swear, have an affair, go shopping? Somehow, you react.

But wait! Did you participate in this change? How? When you slow down and catch your breath, clear your mind, and somewhere find objectivity, you might realize that in some way, you took part in that change. Perhaps you even wanted the change and were aware of it on many levels and possibly even ahead of time. Recalling previous changes, how many were truly sudden or unexpected?

Can you explain why you reacted strongly? Why did you feel stressed about that change?

Was your reaction just a reflex? Reactions are all right, unless they are hurtful. Perhaps you weren't ready for opportunities. Perhaps you did not see opportunity in that change.

Every day is different in some way, large or small. Mostly, we like routine. It can feel easier, safe, relaxed, and, above all, familiar. There can be comfort in routine — maybe even a sense of control.

The results of change are unknown and unfamiliar, and they can be exciting or fearful. Sometimes, we have no control of the size or the timing of the change that comes to us. If we have any control at all, we can begin a big change with little changes that can ripple gradually into bigger change. Sometimes a slow change is less stressful because we have time to adjust and assimilate the change.

Difficult change: Some changes are a shock or surprise. Death, tragedies, fires, floods, change in job or profession, and family breakups are some extremely difficult losses that can create huge changes in our lives.

How will you cope with a difficult change?

What support system do you have in place for yourself? Prayer? Exercise? Talking it over with friends and family? Journalling? Meditation? Support group? Literature? Spiritual practice?

When life feels particularly hard or tiring, I do something to lift my soul.

More about huge losses in chapter seven.

Is good change eluding you?

Does happy change elude you? Sometimes I wonder why bad situations occur, and why I seem to experience some of them over and over again.

Those situations will end when I stop putting myself in them. I know now that a situation will recreate itself until I figure out what I need to learn from it.

Consider that problems, difficulties, and changes do have a good side. In confronting them, we take stock, we reflect on the pros and cons, and inevitably we can step away, having learned something new. Challenges stretch us. What we thought was a problem, could, in fact, integrate meaningfully into our life. Has that happened to you?

Look for opportunities in any challenge or obstacle.

Release judgment about yourself and others. In your mind when you see something new or different, say to yourself, "I do not know you. I would like to get to know you." What is the opportunity here?

***Forming a judgment without knowledge
leads to trouble and misunderstanding.***

***Knowledge, experience, and reflection
can be an opportunity for coping
with change and understanding it.***

CREATIVE PRACTICE

Gradually initiating change

Mix things up . . . change the energy.

Whenever you have changed a habit; or are determined to change a habit; or want to inspire a new outlook; or want to invite new things to happen to you, try:

- Rearranging your furniture and pictures
- Changing routines
- Brushing your hair second, if you usually brush it first
- Eating dessert first
- Taking a new route home
- Trying new accent colours in your home, wardrobe, workplace
- Refreshing your accessories
- Jumping out of bed
- Jumping into bed
- Not talking for one day
- Going for a bike ride first, then mowing the lawn if you have time
- Watching no TV for a week
- Letting the students teach

Add your own ideas.

Coping with change

For this painting exercise, you will need to get some art supplies organized. You will need:

- Medium-weight paper that will hold water-based paint, at least 18 by 24 inches in size. Large paper allows you to use your body and arms in larger strokes.
- Water-based paint: any kind will work—tempera, watercolours, or poster paint
- Two or three large brushes; even house-painting brushes will work

The process for the painting is to be expressive. Follow your body impulses; sense what your body wants to do and how it wants to move.

- While you are setting up and getting ready, begin to hum.
- While continuing to hum, paint your situation with colours and patterns to reflect your situation *before* the change. Don't question colours, choices, or strokes.
- When this painting feels done, or you don't know what else to do—pause.
- Begin another painting with colours and patterns to reflect your situation *after* the change. Don't question colours, choices, or strokes. When this painting feels done, or you don't know what else to do—pause.
- Set the paint and brushes aside for the moment.
- On a separate piece of paper for each painting, answer the following questions.
- Where did you feel stuck?
- What helped you go on?
- What was your experience like throughout this whole process?

After you have completed the journalling, what discoveries did you make?

How important is the "right" decision?

Although this may sound simple, the "right choice" is most often the one that we can say "feels right." These decisions seem to be the easiest. Aside from impulsive decisions, our decisions are usually based on trusting our body, our senses, and ourselves. Experience and knowledge may or may not be an asset. However, what is involved in making decisions is an individual matter. Our goal is to make a choice with clarity and certainty.

But how?

When the choice is not clear to you, or the yes/no of your inner voice isn't clear enough, it might help to reflect carefully and clarify your purpose. If indecision haunts you, taking a small step in one direction could help. Sometimes visualizing that first step also helps. Going slowly is not as scary as jumping into a new situation. A small step can usually be retracted if it does not feel right or work out the way you hoped.

As a thinking person, you already have a developed sense of when a situation feels right or wrong. Whether you act on that sense or intuition is, of course, a personal decision.

Check in with your body senses. How are you feeling?

Gaining confidence in your ability to make decisions comes with growing self-awareness.

Often, much can be gained from reflection on past decisions. Learning to understand yourself makes it easier to put energy toward new opportunities and to shift away from situations that don't feel right and/or feel negative.

Take your time to consider a decision.

Remember that a small step can be retracted.

Most decisions are not final.

No decision is still a decision.

CREATIVE PRACTICE

Questions about choice

It is not unusual to have mixed feelings regarding any personal decision. These mixed feelings can create confusion, hesitation, or an overwhelmed feeling. Even once a decision has been made, second-guessing and self-doubt can creep in. Some decisions have many layers. Most decisions can be done in steps. Usually our initial impulse is the "right" one. Still yourself and try and remember your first impulse. Take your time to understand those layers so you can make a choice with the most clarity possible.

Write down your answers to the following:

- What do I think about my situation?
- What are my choices? (Feel free to list any and all choices that come to mind, judging none, as this is a work list and you empower yourself with choices. The next questions help you to edit those choices.)
- Is this choice good for me now?
- Does this choice come from fear? From anger? From guilt? From love?
- How do I feel emotionally? Physically?
- Is there a better choice for me?
- What do I need?
- Is this choice good for my family?
- Is there a choice that benefits everyone?
- Which options give me the most inner peace?

Visualize each choice and some possible outcomes. How does this choice feel?

Consider the source of each feeling in order to understand rather than defend it. Feelings are real and justifiable. Accept them; understand them.

Is the feeling a fight or flight reaction?

Is this a feeling from a past experience? How far past—recent or childhood?

Is the feeling based on a belief system?

Now, after you have done all this, ask yourself, "Will my choice serve me well and enhance my life (and possibly those around me)?" And again, ask yourself: "Which choice will give me the most inner peace?"

THE NOTION OF "MISTAKES"

The word "mistake" gives perfectionists a great deal of grief. We hate to fail, or to make even a small mistake. Look at that word again. It's made up of two parts: "miss" and "take." Could we consider that a mistake could just be a "take" that was missed? In the movies and theatre there are many takes. Trying something again can refine it, change it, and open up some new ideas. Keep in mind that everyone needs to try things out. That is part of the learning process.

How many times have you chided yourself for making a mistake and missing?

> **On the path of discovery and exploration,
> mistakes are necessary stepping stones.**

Think about the benefits resulting from what you at one point thought was a problem.

Stepping stones on a path are silent reminders to take one step at a time. They provide us with direction and information. If something isn't working out, perhaps it requires reflection. Through trial and error, we can gain wisdom. Take information and experience from the situation, build on this valuable knowledge, and carry on in a different way. As you want the "hits," you must accept the "misses."

> **Successful people keep trying.**

Sometimes the process of achieving a goal or choice has its obstacles. A strong sense of purpose and conviction in your goal will help put one foot in front of the other, one step at a time. What you may see now as an obstacle could turn out to be an opportunity.

You can choose a viewpoint. Choose to believe that mistakes in learning are not bad or wrong. This choice can help you to see that a mistake brings a pause to reflect on possibilities, corrections, or even new directions that could work better. Trust yourself to act responsibly and creatively. Collect your inspirations in your journal or in a separate notebook.

Remember that even nature offers "mistakes" as mutations. Some fall away, while others evolve into a new species.

STUMBLING BLOCKS

How blocks happen

If we are blocked anywhere, we will be blocked everywhere; we stiffen up and become restricted. Inadvertently, we often build emotional blocks to our awareness, sensitivity, perception, intelligence, and happiness. Unknown blocks, especially, can cloud, confuse, mask, and inhibit our thinking. Blocks can create resistance to healthy change and joy. What often helps is a non-verbal and non-threatening form of self-expression that allows us to translate and transform those emotions and words without judgment. The arts offer this opportunity.

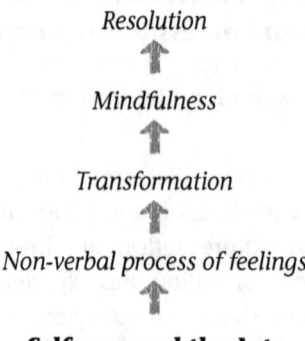

Resolution
⇑
Mindfulness
⇑
Transformation
⇑
Non-verbal process of feelings
⇑
Self-care and the Arts

Expressing feelings and emotions helps to unblock them, often transforming and evolving them into something helpful or practical. There emerges a sense of openness, relaxation, and an energizing receptivity to learning. We can often uncover hidden strengths and resources when we take the time to look for them.

> **To transform blocks and emotions into learning tools that can assist our daily living, it is not necessary to constantly understand or label, analyze, or share them.**

As much as our world is articulated verbally, it also exists non-verbally. This non-verbal world needs to be expressed. The versatility of the arts, for example, lets us express ourselves—without words or unwanted public scrutiny—so that we can find new perceptions.

Getting past those funks and stumps

To be creative and live your best life, you need to be able to think and work freely toward any desire, to gain new habits that nurture your creativity and energy.

There are times when you get depressed or frustrated, and going on seems impossible. I have wanted to quit all types of artistic endeavours several times. This doesn't include all the little times when I had split-second frustrations. Here are some habits that are so common you may scarcely be aware of them. Consider which apply to you and your project.

Wishful thinking

It's just wishful, and accomplishes nothing. To change something takes action. The next time you catch yourself doing some wishful thinking, ask yourself what it is really about. What action could you take to make your desire happen?

Fantasizing to escape your reality

Fantasy is functional for a short while and could even be fun on occasion. But if you really want a situation to be different, then identifying practical steps toward concrete change must be considered.

Living in the future (or the past)

It avoids today, and keeps you from being in the present. Some planning is good. Take time to do serious planning, instead of just daydreaming about it. Daydreaming and wishful thinking are ways of living in the future, not today. If you're thinking that things will be better when such-and-such happens, be aware that such-and-such might never happen. Situations are constantly being introduced and resolved throughout life. Life is here today, right now. Things are the way they are. If your "now" is so wrong, then ground yourself in the present long enough to make serious, practical changes. Avoiding your present, unhappy state will not make it go away.

Feeling flat

Is it possible that your emotions are blocked to avoid feeling pain, fear, or grief? Blocking feelings may be sapping energy from the really important matters that need your energy and attention.

Your blocked emotions need to be recognized and, if necessary, addressed. Can you figure out when and how you came to feel like this? Take time to consider what you can do about it. On the other hand, when you are feeling great, recognizing what does make you feel energetic and happy may give you some clues as to what is lacking when you feel otherwise.

More on blocked emotions on page 121.

Feeling resentful or angry

Any resentment, no matter how small, could be creating resistance to enjoyment or a goal.

Feeling anxious

Anxiety can be so severe that it can inhibit an individual from taking any action toward his goal. If you suspect that you have anxiety, consider seeking professional counselling to assist you. It is something that can be managed.

Qualifying feelings

Part of our humanness is to experience the full spectrum of feelings and emotions. To cover up, suppress, or negate any of these feelings depresses them. This in turn creates blocks, tension, stress, dis-ease, illness, and/or depression.

Once we can recognize them, an empowering way to manage emotions is to define them.

How intense is the emotion? What is the quality of it? Is it useful?

For example, I have been looking at and feeling anxiety differently. When anxiety comes up in my body, as it roils in my stomach, I wonder: Is the source of my anxiety an old story, a belief, or a lie? If it is any of these, once exposed, it dissipates.

If there is a reason or cause for the anxiety, then the anxiety has come as a signal, becoming useful in that I likely need to take action of some sort. As I take action, the anxiety dissipates.

All emotions can be worked with in this way.

If I begin getting angry and impatient while driving in traffic, I remind myself to be present. I need to pay attention to stay as safe as possible. This anger or impatience is mostly a thought or a belief about expectations that are not controllable or very important.

What about anger due to an injustice to children?

What about infatuated love?

What about jealousy?

If you have trouble changing any of these habits, consider professional coaching to assist you.

Setting up a support system

So how can you walk around or jump over those blocks? How can you minimize or avoid them altogether? How can you manage them?

Read and learn

When you are feeling discouraged, seek resources that can support you and inform you. Learn about depression and understand what frustration is. Frequently review the lists and charts you will be making in the creative practices that follow. They might reveal things about yourself that you need to attend to. Reading previous pages in your journal could reveal other low times that you have already faced. What has pulled you past your difficult times in the past?

Act on your ability to choose

There are always choices. A choice, whether it is a belief, a thought, or an action, can affect you positively or negatively. You can wallow in your funk, or you can choose to grab an opportunity by examining the problem or mood from all sides, and reviewing possibilities for change.

Consider downtime as a rest period

I notice that after a holiday, a special event, or some exciting encounter—or a place where I have felt elated, jubilant, joyful, and full of life—my mood shifts to a quieter, restful phase. I always thought of this downtime negatively, even though nothing was really wrong in my life. Now I settle into that downtime, appreciating it for what it is—an opportunity to unwind. By recognizing this, there seems to be less downtime; it passes by quickly and soon I am back skipping along in my life.

Turn a funk into an opportunity for change or improvement

Check your support lists for missing elements. Take quiet time to journal. Describe your feelings to uncover what is niggling at you and then look at choices for change.

Master your own mind

You always have a choice. You can choose to think happy, positive, building thoughts and go to those memory banks where you were joyful and strong. You can choose to focus on the gifts and the opportunities of life. Or you can choose a path of negativity and focus on what you do not have. Be aware of your thought patterns; how the same thoughts can repeat many times. Push them away by self-prompts such as saying,

"Next!" Journal writing is very helpful in processing new thoughts. Decide what you want to experience.

Check out your mental blocks

These are otherwise known as assumptions, suppositions, beliefs, prejudices, and judgments. Do any of the blocks below seem familiar? Add some of your own, then open up your thinking and creativity.

Belief systems that can block your progress

"Play is frivolous."

"To err is wrong."

"I'm not creative."

"I'm not smart."

"I'm too fat!"

"Follow the rules."

"Don't be foolish—this is not practical."

"It costs too much."

"I don't have time for that."

"Those who can't, teach."

Some belief systems are very strong. Some are deeply embedded from childhood, our culture, and our family. These beliefs may be very resistant to moving aside or going away. Another way to manage them is to greet them, embrace them, maybe work with them. What challenges do they present? What opportunities/strengths do they bring?

Blocks to the arts and creativity

Negative beliefs that create a lack of confidence, a sense of competitiveness, unrealistic expectations, and blocked emotions can all inhibit creativity.

Negative beliefs

When you were growing up, did you ever hear, "Your sister has all the artistic talent in the family," or, "You don't have the body of a dancer," or "You sing off-key"? These and many other negative comments can shut you down in your creative pursuits.

Often, as parents, we are career-focused for our children and think that if they do not have enough talent for a career, then it is pointless for them to pursue their love of just being creative, forgetting how important this pursuit is to their livelihood. Growing up, a child remembers those negative comments, but not always where they came from. As adults, we believe we are not capable of drawing or dancing, writing or sculpting, and should not "waste our time" if we will not be good at it. Sometimes, after many years, my students come to me, scared yet driven, to try to reawaken and nurture what got pushed away in their youth. Many others don't even bother to try, believing that they have no aptitude at all.

What cynical onlooker has not asked, "What are you wasting your time on? Isn't there something worthwhile you can do?" Such thoughtless comments can be crushing.

What about the sheer pleasure of being creative? Can this be enough?

Expectations, competitiveness, and commercial success

> **Sometimes there is an expectation of what art should look or sound like, forgetting that there is a whole process of exploration and practice.**

Students can quickly get into a competitive mode of wanting to paint like the teacher, or better than their classmates. Sometimes, they have a goal of wanting to frame or sell the piece, and let expectation and judgment determine what the piece should be. They forget the creative process of just following their hearts.

It is all right to strive for excellence in your field, though focusing on expectations or awards will suppress your connection with what is important to you in your heart. The fear of losing could suffocate pleasure and any aspiration for exploration or inventiveness.

> **The great thing about following your heart and listening to yourself is that your whole being will flourish with energy, and the quality of your life will soar as it unfolds like a great adventure. Earning approval will not be a concern.**

Focusing on commercial success could take you away from your growth as an artist. It will stress you. Your desires and creativity will cower in the shadow of the financial bottom line. How can you dare to take risks and hot, passionate leaps of faith when your thoughts are concerned with the questionable existence of a financial safety net? Fear of failure stifles who we are. Reality says there are no assurances.

If art is your living, you may need to include various types of creative outlets, some for financial gratification, and some just for your own creative gratification.

A few years back, I was stressed about shows and selling. I started to hate painting. Saddened that I could dread my passion, I took a year off from any commercial venture around my art, and gave myself a year to paint only what I wanted, when I wanted. I was surprised to see how open my work became, and the leaps that I made in connecting with my subjects. I was surprised to see the risks and liberties I took. Life was getting juicy again!

Today there are plenty of ideas, and the mornings don't come quickly enough.

Her deepest longing

Her deepest longing:
to stay with the Dreamer
floating though the clouds,
softly taking a path,
making the journey.

Her deepest longing:
excitement,
unbridled enthusiasm,
like a dance of fireworks,
flaring imagination.

Her deepest longing:
to be confident in passion
like a full moon, so bright.
Shadows have meaning
and no one is lost.

Her deepest longing:
to be free of pain
and know true love
like an ocean wave,
endless.

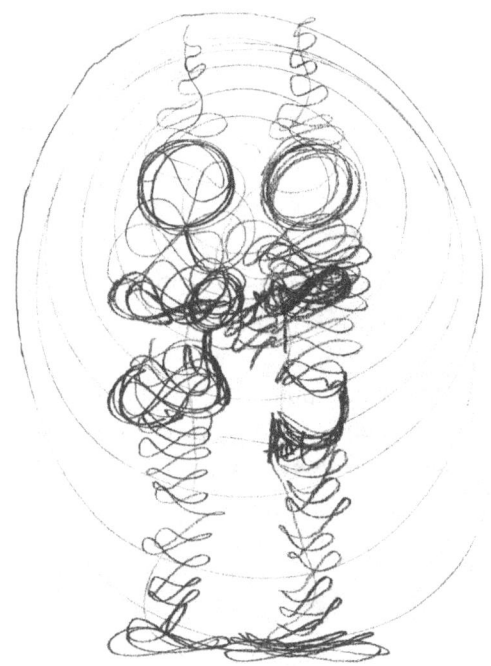

Setting up more support systems

Share with trusted family members or friends
Talking about how you feel can lighten your load, and hearing the experiences of others can often provide valuable suggestions and lessons.

Take time to meditate
In meditation, your mind gains a calm confidence. Slowing down will reveal new thoughts and new approaches.

Write down your dream
Then list what might be stopping you from realizing it.

Write out a detailed plan toward your goal
This plan could include blocks and how to overcome them. There could be small steps and large steps. In between every step, consider smaller

steps. In between those smaller steps, insert mini-steps. This exercise might seem trivial, but hang in there. Be persistent. Remember: one drop at a time fills that bucket.

- Make a list of support systems and slowly implement them.
- Seek relationships with like-minded people.
- Determine how you could take better care of yourself.
- Discover what resources could support you; what knowledge could serve you best.
- Put ideas, thoughts, and responsibilities where they belong.
- Start with one mini-step today.

Write out changes that will happen when you realize your goal. Then write how you will feel when you realize your goal. Read these daily. As your mind gets familiar with these ideas, you will recognize and attract these things into your life.

Pray

What is prayer?

Prayer can be done in many ways for many purposes. Prayer can be done in different styles: pleading, bargaining, admitting, giving gratitude, giving, blessing and requesting are a few. A prayer can be addressed to the God of your understanding, to Allah, Great Spirit, Shiva, Krishna, to nature, healing energy, and so on.

A prayer can be a mantra, an affirmation, a practice .

A prayer can be a meditation, a concentration on kindness or sending love.

A prayer can be an earnest hope or wish.

Pray alone, pray together in a group, and ask for prayers.

Every facet of self-care raises your
life condition higher and higher!

CREATIVE PRACTICE

Discovering your blocks

Check off those blocks that feel familiar and, in some cases, justified.

Competition	Time
Money	Lack of knowledge
Opinion	Lack of gratification
Lack of support	Distractions
Fear	Rituals
Belief systems	Habits
Cultural beliefs	Patterns
Judgment	Perfectionism
Fear of change	Fear of failure
Fear of success	Addiction
Obsessions	Resentments
Work ethic	Overwork
Emotional blocks, walls, fears	Wanting to be perfect
Wanting the project to be "right"	Policies, rules, procedures, protocol

Name and describe what you believe is standing in the way of your dreams, your creativity, or loving your life. If your block is missing from the list, add it.

Consider the blocks you defend.

Make a list of ways to eradicate all or part of a block with the resources you have today. Include in that list the steps you can take in the next few days, in the next few weeks, and even months ahead.

What one small step can you take now?

If you have trouble articulating your blocks and steps, try using the creative practices "Facing the Dragon" and "Block Busters" on the following pages.

CREATIVE PRACTICE

Facing the Dragon

What would you *need* to face the Dragon?

Are you holding back on something you do not want to face? Perhaps this is a clear signal to look at that challenge in depth. What can you learn here? Ask yourself these questions and write your answers.

- Do you know what stresses you?

- Is it confrontation?

- Is it financial?

- Is it commitment?

- Is it the unknown results of any type of change?

- What is it that you don't want to experience?

- What experience will help to overcome it?

- What is it that you are afraid will happen?

- Is there a problem?

- What would help you overcome the fear?

- What might change in your life?

- What is there to gain or lose?

- Will you have to accept something?

- Will it affect your family life?

- Will it affect your work?

- Does it challenge your belief system? Is it possible that one of these answers is creating resistance to overcoming a block and pursuing a dream?

Block Busters

- Is a block stopping you from pursuing a dream?

- Is it manageable or unmanageable? State how in either case.

- What would small steps look like?

- What step can you take now toward surpassing your block to be closer to your dream?

- What step can you take tomorrow?

- Can you take the time to imagine how it would feel when you reached your goal?

- Can you take the time to imagine how it would feel once you overcame your block?

- What step can you take this week?

- What step can you take this month?

- How will you support yourself?

- Who and what will support you with your steps?

- Is there someone you can share your goals with?

Stimulating your perceptions

Begin by answering what you can in point form.
- Try journalling as described on pages 42 to 44.
- Try painting the essence of your block.
- Try painting the essence of your goal.

Describe the differences and similarities in these two paintings. How can these differences and similarities relate to any of your notes on blocks?

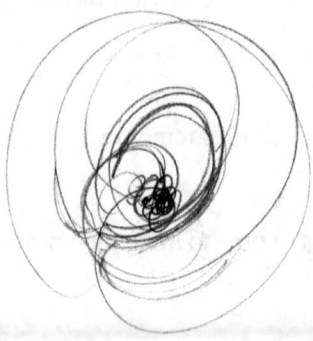

Courage, my friend.

It takes courage to be honest with yourself and others.

THE MANY ASPECTS OF STRESS AND CREATIVITY

In art and in life, stress is subjective. It can evoke excitement and challenge, and it can also invoke illness, exhaustion, and despair.

If stress inhibits or harms, then it has gotten too big and needs attention. We all differ in how stress affects us and which stresses affect us. That is why it is important for each of us to assess positive or negative stress triggers and to create a personal balance for ourselves.

Stress can result from emotional, mental, physical, or environmental factors, and sometimes any combination of the four.

Take stock of your own stress triggers and find ways to eliminate them or to lessen their impact. What stresses are you feeling today? How could you ease that stress load right now? Stresses change. As life progresses and you evolve, prior stresses may dissipate.

Assess your working and home environment. Is your body being stressed from second-hand smoke, pollution, noise, fumes, water chemical treatment, drugs, alcohol, caffeine, inadequate or harsh lighting, variations in air pressure, stale air, or other chemicals such as perfumes, cleaners, and solvents?

Review your relationships with others and work to improve them. If that's not possible, consider how you can minimize the negative effects these relationships have on you.

We cannot control all elements in our world, but some stresses can be eliminated or managed. Do what you can. Remember that each negative stress weakens you, just as every positive one strengthens you.

To feel refreshed, vital and healthy, taking care of our physical health is important. This next section is merely a brief note to ask you to notice certain areas in physical selfcare. As some of these areas may resonate with you, then I invite you to research them further. There are many books and resources that address each area in depth and quite thoroughly.

Taking care of your physical body

This is where you live. If this body breaks down, where else are you going to live?

It makes sense that a healthy body will have more energy and be more vital. A healthy body is important for a healthy mind, and a healthy mind is important for a healthy body. Machinery mistreated or lacking repair breaks down in time. Like any machine, your body needs proper maintenance, fuel, and care. The following points are a simple invitation for you to consider the well-being of your physical body.

Eat right

Healthy food is imperative for happy, balanced, creative living. Quality food must be a priority. To function well, our bodies need fresh foods free of pesticides and additives. Continued weariness and lack of energy could be caused by poor diet and resorting to artificial stimulants. How much processed sugar and caffeine are in your diet?

Drink lots of water

Drink a minimum of fourteen ounces of water per day. Your body, especially kidneys and liver, need water to help flush toxins from your system. Tea and other liquids are not the same as plain, clear, delicious water. Your body doesn't need to filter water and can flush toxins more easily and quickly with water than with other liquids.

Exercise

Exercise for energy. This doesn't mean becoming an athlete. It means keeping active with walks, bicycle riding, swimming, tai chi, yoga, dancing, playing with children or grandchildren, gardening, stretching, or working. Keeping all your parts agile and moving easily keeps you in shape for most of the activities and expectations of your life. Exercise stimulates happiness and well-being. If you are feeling blue, take a brisk, one-hour walk and notice the difference in how you feel.

Rest

Are you getting enough sleep? Good sleep means restful, uninterrupted sleep. If you could sleep as long as you liked, how long would you sleep? Do you regularly drag yourself out of bed via an alarm, and stimulate your body with caffeine to get going? How often do you consume sugar-loaded or refined foods during the day for energy? Listen to your body.

Are you suffering from insomnia? Is stress making you sleepless? Or is the insomnia stressing your body? Insomnia has different causes, such as diet, medical or social problems, trauma, environment, stimulants, overtiredness, and alcohol consumption. Listen to your body for clues. Investigate your reactions to the possible causes. For me, I find that chocolate, any amount of caffeine, the computer, terrifying movies before bed, and exciting plans ahead are triggers for my restless nights.

Try some relaxation techniques. See what works for you.

Regular exercise will also help to promote sound sleep.

Brush your skin

The skin is the body's largest organ, so skin care is important for optimum health. Dry-brushing your skin daily removes dead skin flakes. By dry-brushing your skin, it can breathe easier, and toxins are released more readily.

Dry brush technique

Use a natural bristle body brush or a dry, stiff loofah sponge. Gently brush in circular motions, moving up the body. You will feel tingly, alive, and refreshed. Let your skin breathe further by putting only natural, breathable fabrics next to it.

> **Caring for our physical body enhances our mental state and our general health.**

Taking care of yourself

It is hard to be balanced when you are fuelled on junk food and stimulants and lack sleep. Physical depletion affects the mental and emotional capabilities of the mind.

Be selfish in caring for yourself. It is the only body you have and it has to last a lifetime! Nurture yourself by building and supporting the person you are. Believe in yourself and you will thrive. As you nourish, heal, encourage, and comfort yourself, you will be more able to give the same to others.

Your emerging happiness and actions will touch everything in your daily life. The energy you exude can ripple through to your family, your neighbourhood, and your community and country. To seek knowledge and truth takes courage. It may be an easier road to slide along on the surface, but it's a little slimy, too.

To embrace life is fulfilling and terrifying all at once. But always worth it! Do you like roller coaster rides?

Humour and play

Have a laugh during the day. Read some comic books, make a laugh list, watch a funny movie, collect favourite cartoons, and decorate your workplace. Have fun!

Too often we become bunged up in our routine or task, taking ourselves too seriously. Then we forget where we came from and what we really are doing here. Humour frees us up. It heals us and lightens our load.

Play is worthwhile. Play is healing. Laughter is healing.

> *Play and fun are powerful motivators*
> *for creative thought and genius.*
> *Play loosens, livens, and opens us up.*

Play gives us a break from serious routine. It stimulates our neuropathways in new ways.

Take time to play. You, your family, and your work will benefit.

Ideas will literally pop out of your brain while you are frolicking in the water, chasing your children around the house, or playing tag with your dog. Or maybe it's your hobby . . . beading, cooking, gardening? What brings you joy? What brings you laughter?

Try it—you'll like it and you'll be productive in other areas of your life as well.

Really!

Challenge and Change

CREATIVE PRACTICE

Making your own sample laugh list.

What makes me laugh:
- Tickling my son
- Dancing in the rain
- Making up a language and then asking people for directions
- Eating without utensils
- Singing the hokey-pokey
- Popping popcorn without a lid
- A baby eating chocolate pudding

Creative holiday

For those stress triggers over which you and I have little control, a dose of creativity helps to lighten the mood, change the scene, and refresh the mind.

Shifting to a creative activity for a time is rather like shifting gears.

> ***Experiencing the arts—music, dance, painting, and so on—can help the body and mind to transcend blocked emotions and memories and lessen tension and stressful periods.***

It can also help return you to your "normal" self. A period of creativity can be as rejuvenating as a nap.

Do you feel stuck?

Do you feel creatively stifled, trapped? Becoming aware of your mental traps is the first step to getting free of them.

- Ask yourself: How practical am I? Is being practical a priority?
- Is my work routine, logical, cost-effective, and/or average?
- What if I tried something out of the ordinary today? Would it feel crazy? Out of control?
- What would happen?

Try not to be judgmental of your new idea or different action. Mix one day up as a holiday from your routine. Have some fun. You will have changed your energy flow.

Do you always follow the rules of procedure, the guidelines for techniques, or the same order in your work? Break a pattern: Break any one pattern or break a lot of them. Challenge yourself.

- Do a task in a different order.
- Do a task in a different way. What would your problem (or task) look like from someone else's perspective? How would you look if you were performing your task while holding a banana? Play it through in your mind. Sometimes a silly or funny idea can break us out of our seriousness.
- Try something new.
- Learn a new skill, then practise it.

- Take a risk. Risk feeling foolish, or just looking foolish. Risk having fun.
- Dream up a new possibility. Ask yourself, "What if?"

There is not just one approach. Avoid falling in love with one inspiration. Know that there are many "right" approaches.

One of my good teachers, Bill Bayley, asked us for ten solutions to a design problem. When the whole class moaned, he reminded us all that there are hundreds of approaches to that particular design problem alone. He had witnessed that each time he handed out the same exercise—year after year.

Solutions, innovations, transformations, and ideas are all out there. Let's discover and develop them.

Chaos

What is your comfort level with chaos? I don't like chaos in music; however, when I jam in our community drumming circle, the chaos circles us until we entrain with each other and create some phenomenal musical piece.

The more familiar I am with chaotic situations, the more comfortable I am.

I see chaos as a natural way of being. Chaos is more a process of becoming than a state. Nature, weather, people, and life are all chaotic and usually find a place of balance and flow.

Donald Winnicott and Garth Turner saw chaos as very creative. I agree also with Stephen Levine when he says this state of formlessness through an immersion of the arts brings situations, new metaphors, and new perspectives.[1]

Already our lives tend to be overly busy and chaotic. Our resistance to enter formlessness and unfamiliar territory is understandable, although with art in a supportive environment, we can learn the possibility of some sense of order and balance.

> *The times in which we live, the rapid pace of life, the explosion of information, the expansion of technology, and the destruction of the natural environment are real aspects of a world that is both exciting and disturbing. We are living in chaos. Art making, living poesies, is the only thing that makes any sense as a way of trusting in a larger and multidimensional whole.*[2]

Chaos in the arts can be illustrated by describing a community drumming group I belong to. The drummers start with their own rhythm and create a chaotic soundscape with what appears to contain little or no rhythmical relationship. Gradually, the rhythmical influences converge in a harmonious piece. It appears that the strongest rhythms converge to maintain a repeated and recognizable beat.

I have noticed that in the elementary school classroom, chaos does not sustain itself for long, and the group self-organizes itself. When I would go in to provide art sessions, the classrooms were bedlam, whether it

---

1 S.K. Levine, *Principles and Practices of Expressive Arts Therapy* (London: Kingsley, 2005), 48–51.
2 Sally Atkins, *Expressive Arts Therapy: Creative Process in Art and Life* (Parkway Publishers, 2003), 25.

was Grade 3, 4, or 5. Children were excited from their recess and were clambering over each other to see what I had brought. I would hand out mini-chores, and in a short while, the classroom-studio space was set up, with the children engaged, orderly, and eager for further instruction.

Another example was a group of female teens struggling with classroom absenteeism in their high school. They began by arriving late, fully engrossed in social chatter; then they would slowly gather around the circle to munch on snacks. I would let the conversations carry on, curious to hear what they talked about, since they did not mind my presence. Usually within ten to fifteen minutes, one or two of them said, "So what are we doing today?" and that was the beginning of the session. By that time, they were ready, settled in, and fully engaged. Their attendance rate was extremely high for my sessions, which the school saw as a miracle, since these young women rarely attended class. About after five or six sessions of the ten-week workshop, these women were regularly attending their other classes as well.

Many people, especially teachers, seem fearful of chaos. Their training is "all-eyes-on-me" before the class begins. I see them use much energy, by harsh voices and disciplinary measures, to try and rein in young spirits that are lively and energized and/or have been traumatized at some time in their lives. Naturally, the youth do not respond compliantly as they revert to their own coping mechanisms of rebellion or disassociation.

I see that we try to control our environment and establish order in an effort to stay away from chaos. There is a tendency to fear the unpredictable and the uncontrollable. We do this by redefining unique experiences, categorizing and reconstructing reoccurring aspects and regularities. In doing so, we are in danger of rigidity and petrifaction.

I agree with Kriz:[3] When we control and stay stagnant, nothing can move or be created.

In a recent workshop at a local public school, the participating musician surprised me by trying to push and force the traumatized children to stand orderly and quietly in line. He would sternly bark out demands for performance and threaten punishment. When they did finally attempt to stand in line, he complicated the task with an additional task of standing tallest to largest, which ensured more bedlam. The order he was trying to create perpetuated the unruliness. He finally gave up, and they filed down the hallway. Another day, when he was not there, we

---

[3] Jurgen Kriz, "On Attractors," *Poiesis, A Journal of the Arts and Communication* (1999).

began a string spiderweb on the floor with the children as they scattered in from recess. They were given the opportunity of self-regulating, and entered the session. One by one, they all joined the circle to hold the string to create a spider's web. The task was simple and did not demand control, resulting in a lighthearted, fully engaged circle check-in and a more engaged session.

In my art, in order to paint wet-in-wet watercolours, I have to give in to the chaos of unpredictable chemical reactions and weather conditions; I have to give up controlling the process and outcome and let the watercolours paint themselves. Then I work with what comes up in the images and the surprises that happen. The most pleasing part of it for me is when I see my painting crystallize before me.

Personally, chaos can feel difficult, unknown, and unfamiliar, which might translate into feeling unsafe and uncertain. In chaos, it is hard to be relaxed, bored, lazy, and dreaming. Chaos engages our senses and captivates us so that we are fully present.

Think about it: Are you ever totally relaxed and daydreaming in chaotic situations?

Next time you are in a chaotic situation, breathe and take it in as an observer. Watch the dynamics. For certain you'll experience creativity.

Life is a smorgasbord

Some days you might just want dessert.

Some days you want to try everything.

Some days you want meat and potatoes.

Appetite fluctuates. Honour your appetite. In everything that you do—workshops, practices, techniques, beliefs—choose from the smorgasbord of life and assemble your plate to suit your tastes and appetite for today.

Don't hesitate to explore, learn, study, and grow in unexpected ways and at different times.

Sometimes you need to explore with your intuition and sometimes you might want a guide.

Listen to yourself and to what you need.

Everything in our life is related
to everything else.

Even the seemingly intangible aspects
of your new creatuve direction will
creep into your other routines,
suffusing them with new energy and insight.

TAKING CHARGE OF YOUR THOUGHTS

Do what you love. Follow your heart. Follow your joy!

We all have special gifts, and there is something that we each do uniquely, well, and easily.

Honour your work—simple, large, small, complicated, dull, and/or fancy.

Believe that you are worthwhile.

When you have love and passion for your work, believe in the quality, service, and love that you bring to it.

What you give will always be returned.

Be open to seeing your goals and dreams unfold—in the most unlikely way. Go with the flow. Accept situations as they come with ease, realizing that you can neither predict nor control everything.

Be hopeful.

Be creative. Being creative means being open to possibilities and probabilities. Be open to them. Your desires will be fulfilled more than you could have imagined.

Hold onto that vision! Define your purpose by writing out your dream, your vision, or your intentions. Seeing them in writing underlines purpose, provides meaning, and instills enthusiasm.

Be thankful. Feeling thankfulness and appreciation brings serenity and happiness to our lives.

Becoming aware of your thoughts

We are more than our brain. Our brain functions on the history of memory and experience.

> *Our minds are often cluttered with random thoughts. Be aware of repetitive, negative, and unyielding inner chatter.*

Some negative thoughts include all-or-nothing thinking, black-and-white thinking, jumping to conclusions, or making rash assumptions.

Sometimes past problems, taking situations personally, and blaming yourself or others inappropriately crowd out positive reflections, overlook the roles and responsibilities of others, or might fail to consider the whole picture.

Be aware of uncompromising mind chatter and edit it accordingly. It takes practice to do this, so be patient with yourself. Notice when your inner critic is attacking you. Does it seem to happen most when you are tired? Hungry? Are the thoughts a habit? Does it occur in the company of certain people? What are your triggers? Often, such thoughts gang up on you when you have excluded the positive elements in your life by focusing on what was lost instead of what is available.

Try looking at each situation differently. Reword your thinking. With practice, you will quickly identify mind comments that are not serving you and you can quickly delete them. Be easy on yourself, because some of these thought patterns and "mind tapes" may be imbedded and resist your attempts to unseat them. Gradually, through your awareness of their negativity, you will be able to identify self-defeating mind ramblings and "set them on a shelf" or delete them.

Making yourself aware of negative thoughts makes it possible for you to edit them accordingly.

Scheduling your drama and worry time

Worrying can be very useful if it means looking at a problem from different sides and coming up with solutions. However, worrying is not useful if your thoughts go round and round in circles. It becomes a fruitless activity that wastes time and energy.

Scheduling your worrying can turn it from being wasteful to fruitful. Here's a two-step approach that I use.

1. Don't fight it.

Instead of worrying off and on all day long, I will allot myself ten to twenty minutes to wallow in the depths of worry and drama.

When I first tried giving in to those "down" feelings — but only for a set time — I set a timer. However, I rarely used the full time because I did not need it. By permitting myself to deliberately focus on those feelings rather than fighting them, I soon got bored.

Now I can judge when my time invested in worry or despair is enough, and am able to move on and experience what the rest of the day has to offer.

2. Make worrying an assignment.

This works best if you work on this assignment half an hour per day and start worrying deliberately. Find a quiet spot where you can write undisturbed. Take a pen and paper and write down everything that comes to mind. In my private practice my clients and I call this the "dumping journal". Try if possible to write at the same time of the day. Attach it to your already established routine, like a morning coffee or tea.

If possible choose a moment that allows you to relax and distract yourself afterwards.

You will notice that the conscious effort of the worrying sessions makes thinking in circles almost impossible. Writing your worries down reinforces this further. Nobody wants to write down the same thoughts 12 times. This forces the thoughts to go in a different direction and frequently stops them from looping.

As you write you may also find yourself fleshing out the problems and coming up with solutions — another benefit of scheduling worry time.

In the event your brain begins to worry again, be firm and remind yourself that you have written the worries down, and this is all you can do at the moment about the worrying situations. Then change your thoughts to another topic.

You will notice that your brain will get tired of concentrated worry and will let those worry thoughts go.

You are responsible for yourself

Take 100 percent responsibility for your life.

When you blame someone or something outside of yourself for making you feel a certain way, you are giving up your power over yourself.

When you take responsibility for your own thoughts and feelings, you take back your power because you are choosing how you are going to think.

Be in control of your own thoughts and not a victim of external influences.

COMMUNICATING MINDFULLY WITH OTHERS

Listening, speaking, watching, feeling—how attentive are you when communicating with others? Are you respectful and thoughtful? Do you assume that others automatically understand what you intend to communicate?

The power of words

It is your responsibility to communicate clearly and, in turn, attend carefully to communication addressed to you. Give others the attention you would like to receive.

> *Often it is our preoccupation*
> *with expressing our own ideas*
> *that can leave us less responsive to others.*

An important aspect of communication is not only what we express but how we are expressing it. While at some level we understand the difference between inspirational and positive language and words that hurt, control, or denigrate, we don't always put that knowledge into practice.

Over the past few years, while instructing teachers on perception skills, I have noted the many long faces mirroring shocked recognition of how often they had inadvertently discouraged, suppressed creativity, and even dampened children's developmental success by their own insensitive, judgmental language and perhaps even by words intended as jokes. Adults, too, can be hurt by words hurled with little thought.

Diligent awareness will help you make positive adjustments to your ways of communication, not just in the words you use, but also in body language, general mannerisms, and, perhaps most of all, in your ability to listen.

Respectful language habits are critical in developing self-esteem and self-respect, and will eventually influence others to consider how they are communicating. Learning, sharing, encouraging, and negotiating conflict resolution are then workable, accessible, and flowing—to everyone's benefit.

Words that discourage

We are well-meaning in our intentions to compliment, praise, and joke. Yet some words and phrases can be so final, relentless, and unforgiving that they are discouraging and demoralizing. Jokes are really not funny when they demean someone else. Nor are harsh tones or sarcasm constructive or motivating.

Sometimes in self-talk we can set ourselves up for failure or disappointment by using competitive and evaluative terms. Some of these are judgment-type words that put you or someone else in a category.

Words that tend to label, measure, evaluate, or command can be misconstrued as judgmental, limiting, controlling, or even condemning:

always	never	impossible	have to
should	can't	must	regret
guilt	if only	supposed to	ought to
difficult	doubt	but	

Words that inspire competition and grading could be potential set-ups for failure depending on the connotation and situation:

good	bad	better	best	great

Words that instill frustration or fear of failure require careful consideration, especially where there are no absolutes, such as in performance and creativity:

complicated	difficult	right	correct
accurate	mistake	wrong	incorrect
error	cheat	unacceptable	hard
easy	mess		

Take a moment to think about the pressure these words can place on anyone. To introduce a subject as "easy" or "difficult" assumes a value judgment that might not be shared. Consider, instead, whose standard is being presented. Introducing a subject as "new" or "fascinating" is more approachable and inspires curiosity. Because of differing abilities, some tasks take varying effort and time. Individuality needs to be accounted for.

Let's be loud so then we can be quiet.
Let's be quiet so we can be loud.

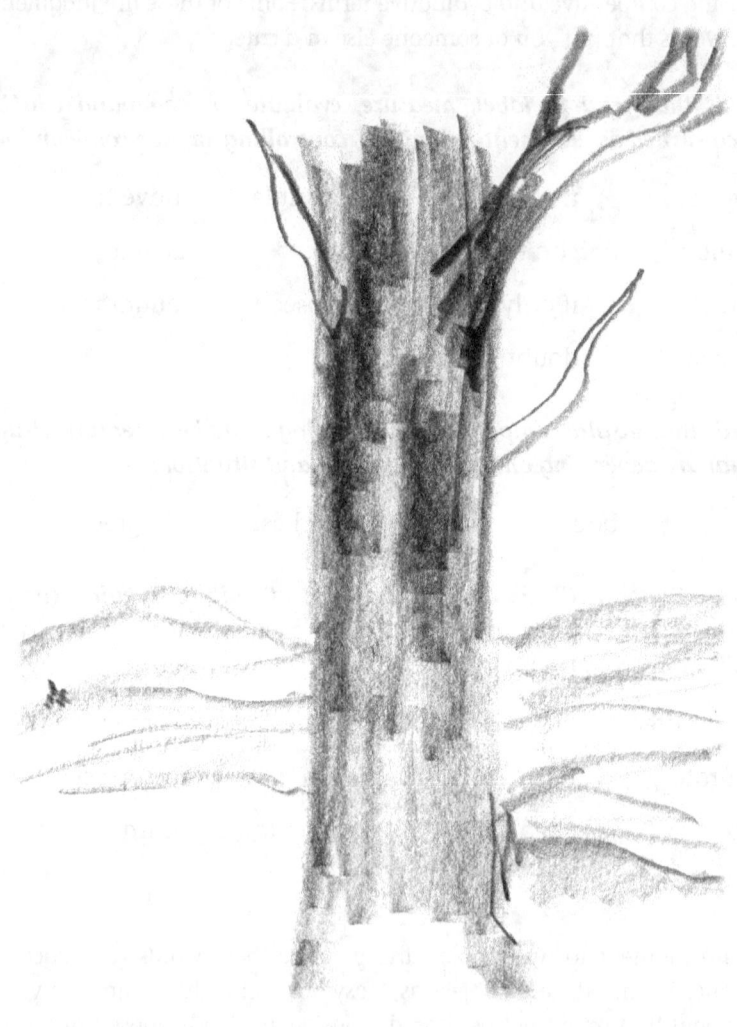

Words that encourage

How can you be encouraging? How can you guide, develop, enhance? These questions are not just for teachers in a classroom, but apply to all our relationships with others.

- Acknowledge the validity of someone's statement and his or her right to say it.
- Be aware of your words and their impact.
- Respond and praise sincerely; encourage while offering guidance

Sometimes, explaining your viewpoint and choice of words can soften necessary criticism or correction. Take care to use words appropriately. The following are some suggestions on building words and comments.

- In taking responsibility, try using "I" statements for opinions and feelings.
- When talking about personal tasks and opinions, try to appreciate differences and uniqueness without the necessity of agreement or disagreement.
- Think about it.
- Try it.

Here are a few examples:

- I like the way you are working.
- That's an interesting way of looking at it.
- You have figured that out!

Make a list of your own examples.

The external critic

After a well-meaning friend called supposedly to "encourage" me, I felt terrible. I was a wreck. She spoke of my true potential and how I had not gone far enough, and that what I was currently doing was not enough. She noted that I have a great deal to offer and must get it out there.

For several days, I mulled over that call. If it was supposed to be acknowledging my great potential, why did I feel so bad?

Reflecting later with a friend who'd had a similar experience, I realized that the message of the call was about my coming short of who she thought I could be. There was disparagement rather than helpfulness in her tone and words.

> *It's wonderful when people*
> *believe in you and your greatness.*
> *It's even more potent when you believe in yourself.*

True encouragement comes gently and builds esteem. Suggestive comments could prompt defensiveness. When you can acknowledge your success and growth to please yourself, then you have the most power, because this power emanates from you.

More than language

Various words and meanings can be unclear in any language. Consider the words you use with care. Be open to clarifying, redefining, and reconsidering them.

Consider the framework from which you speak: You are using words from your experience, which may not be the same in another culture or situation.

Articulating can be challenging, regardless of how big your vocabulary is, as words alone can be limiting. Tone, body language, and expression add dimension to what is communicated.

Framing, introducing, offering, and being curious are gentle ways to approach communication. Set an intention to be caring and approachable.

Is a seed any less a seed
when it is first planted?

The value of the journey is in
itself, not the destination.

We just are and are becoming
as we journey through life.

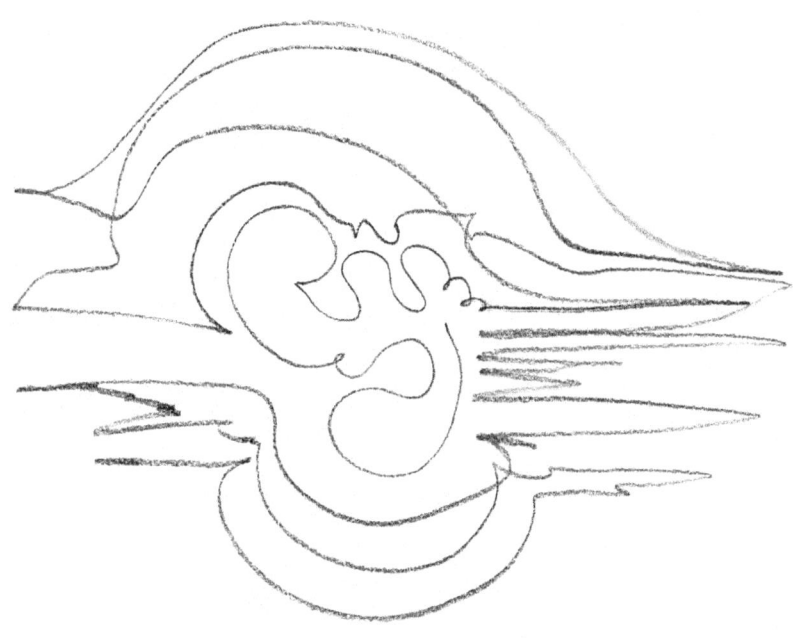

chapter four

BUILDING A MOUNTAIN

Listen to your intuition.

Use your intuition.

That is the way to knowledge.

KNOWING YOURSELF

From the time you were born, you were learning to know and to adapt to the world around you. This outward focus seems to predominate as we grow to adulthood and take on increasing responsibilities.

Isn't it time to get to know the most important person—you? How can you get to know yourself?

- Take time to slow down.
- Set aside quiet time.
- Practise deep breathing and reflection.
- Discover and experience the many forms of meditation, such as singing, chanting, moving, dancing, prayer, and regular journalling.
- Enjoy times of silence.
- Enhance your own knowledge by increasing attentiveness to others and reflecting on your learning from each encounter.
- Think about each relationship and its impact on yourself.
- Reflect on situations (at work and at home) that left you feeling good about yourself or unhappy about yourself. Then take time to figure out why you felt that way.
- Express what you learn about yourself by writing in your journal.

Listen to the voice that drives you,
supports you, and inspires you.

What makes your load lighter and brighter?
What songs cheer you?
What soothes your most intimate fears?

Hero, I hear you today.
I will carry you in my pocket
And like a rainbow you will embrace me
through my day.

Choosing a holistic approach

We stand on shaky ground if all our concerns centre on learning business skills, dressing for success, studying conflict management, team building, and strategic planning. These are all outward-looking goals. How can we advance in any sphere of our life if we do not build a solid inner foundation for ourselves first?

Everything in your life is connected to everything else. When you are whole, healthy, and clear in your thinking and your feelings, then you will be living up to your true potential, personally and professionally, and you will love your life!

Developing and exercising choice

You were born inquisitive, creative, and pure. As you grew, you lived through a variety of experiences, storing memories along the way. Most memories proved helpful, but some could be hurtful even years later, blocking your creativity, diminishing your self-confidence, and stunting your learning and development.

> *You always have a choice. Believing that you have a choice means that you can choose to manage those blocks that stunt your development.*

Everyone possesses strengths and weaknesses, dysfunction and brilliance. You can choose to blame your mistakes on others, and unhappy situations on your dysfunction. There are always many excuses for floundering and failing.

But you always have a choice.

When you say to yourself, "I am not creative," or "I am not artistic," or "I am not a good learner," your own belief is a block against achievement. With such an attitude, how can you stand a chance for fulfillment and happiness? Our inner creativity has no chance with this attitude.

You can choose to aspire to brilliance, to embrace life, and to act now to make the best of your situation. You can choose to grasp opportunities with gusto.

Practise saying to yourself, "I am creative and I can do it!"

When you believe it, then you will do it.

Believe it!

My goal is to discover and to understand how I react to my life experiences and then to be gentle with myself.

In this way, no matter where I am on my journey, I will always be living life to the fullest.

The first day of your life

You have probably heard the familiar saying, "How would you live if you knew that this was to be the last day of your life?"

- Consider living as if every day were your first day. What would be different in the feeling of the "now" experience?
- On this first day, be serious about taking time to relax from the rush to release your sense of playfulness and childlike curiosity. That could be fun!
- How you feel about yourself, your relationships, and your environment is always reflected in your attitude and your emotions. These profoundly affect your health and ability to work, learn, and be creative.
- Caring for yourself permits you and your creativity to be what it is.
- Feel.
- Be.

Is money the answer?

Imagine if you had all the money you need or want, what would your days be like?

- Would you do the same work the same way?
- Would you have and enjoy the same hobbies?
- Would you paint the same way?
- What would you try?
- Would you create the same things?
- Would you live as you do?
- What would your relationships be like?

Ponder these questions when you are alone, perhaps on a long walk. The answers you give yourself might surprise you.

Enthusiasm

- Where is that wellspring of enthusiasm?
- What gives you that burst of energy and excitement?
- Where do you find your zest for life? Is it in the garden? Is it in praying, chanting, singing, or dancing? Playing with children? Is it skiing in the sunshine? Note times when you feel energetic and invigorated. Make a list and pin it up until you know it by heart.

CREATIVE PRACTICE

Being with a child

Give a gift to a child you know—an afternoon or a day to be with you. Then, together, do everything he or she plans. Try it! Get on the floor, climb up a tree, or skip through a secret alley. Sneak off to the corner store and buy a bag of candy. Playful times together can be an amazing treat for both of you. Just let go and enjoy.

Ask a child to name the things she enjoys doing with you. This may take some time, especially if this is a new idea. Be patient and remember you can always add to the list.

Remember when you were a child. What did you like to do? Try to think of twenty things. Then try to do one of these things each day until you've gone through your list. Again, your list may grow, and you might want to do one thing more than once. Go for it. Try it!

Letting go and staying grounded

The experience of just letting go, being with a child, and acting childlike can teach us so much. Did you really try it? Were you surprised to find that it was really fun? Were you surprised by what you learned about yourself?

How can you make sure that you don't lose yourself? How do we not lose ourselves to love, to our relationships, to our job, to our passions?

Try to give only half of yourself away. The other half needs to be planted solidly within you, supported with nurturing and spirituality to enable you to continue giving that other part of yourself away.

Keep yourself grounded and healthy, so that you can continue giving. Giving of yourself and losing yourself are two different things.

Determination and intention

Anything is possible.

> *As a child, I knew that anything was possible,
> and in that certainty it was true.*

As I grew older, I began doubting the miracles of life, the awesome energy and power in our universe. I started to ration my wishes and to curtail my hopes and dreams. This probably happened gradually as I listened to all the conflicted feelings around me.

For many years, I distracted myself from my art. I sold diapers, painted signs, scooped ice cream, and cleaned floors—all the while just dabbling in art. Art was my healing.

Slowly, I became aware that this grown-up insecurity was undermining what I really wanted to accomplish. As an experiment, I decided to revert to my childhood beliefs and, step by step, I regained confidence with the recognition that the source of creativity was not "out there" but was within me.

There have been many ups and downs, and four significant times when I felt so discouraged that I wanted to give up my art altogether, especially as a career. It was only when I accepted my vacillating process—realizing that ups and downs, confidence and discontent are really just the normal stuff of life—that I became free to enjoy doing art. Today, I explore myself through painting, drumming, dancing, and writing. Now I know that I will continue creating.

> *I believe that each person has a well of creativity
> and an ability to achieve dreams.
> It is within us, waiting to be recognized.
> With clarity and confidence of mind, body, and spirit,
> we can access all possibilities.*

Life can be filled with fretful situations. I will choose to pull, to hold, and to attract goodness. Each good thought, each good action ripples outward and profoundly affects others, and like a boomerang comes back to me.

As I continue creating good thoughts and actions for myself, I know that I will be creating goodness for my children, family, community, and the planet.

Building self-confidence

Often the task of learning something new makes us feel awkward. In that awkwardness and unfamiliarity linger the fear of the unknown, fear of failure, and sometimes even the fear of success.

Try breathing through these feelings, accepting them as they arise, and taking small steps forward. Remember to always honour yourself. Listen to yourself. Be gentle with yourself and take your own time. If you get discouraged, try something else. Slowly, as your familiarity grows with the learning of new skills, confidence will replace fear.

Life is about flow and motion.

You can choose how you are going to manage any situation. Will you flap around? Will you create some momentum and then go with the flow? It is up to you to keep paddling until you reach your destination. Up to you—no one else.

Decide how you will travel. Decide whether you want to chase the moose against the current, or smell the sweet pines along the way.

And the good news is that "the journey" is happening right now.

Every day.

Developing supportive tools

Fill your own toolbox with tools that make you feel good. These can include mental, physical, sensual, or spiritual thoughts, activities, rituals, sayings, lists, and so on. Combining one or more supportive tools increases their effectiveness. You may find that some tools are familiar, but with unfamiliar tools, it may just be a matter of recognizing that they are there; or perhaps it will involve teaching yourself something new. Unfamiliar tools take practice, like any new skill.

Know that we all have differing strengths. If you are doing the exercises in this book with a friend or in a group, support each other's strengths and weaknesses with compassion. Try, risk, experiment, experience, and keep practising.

Discover your weaknesses and know that these have the potential to be strengthened; recognize that weaknesses represent an opportunity for your learning and growth.

Remember, the more you enjoy a supportive tool or exercise, the more you'll want to use and keep it in your life and practise it. So, collect a lot of fun support tools to help you through the challenging times.

My vision is clear.

My spirit feels clean.

Today I celebrate an awareness,
and my total awe,

of creation, of which I am a part.

My excitement is in this flow of
energy of what I see and feel.

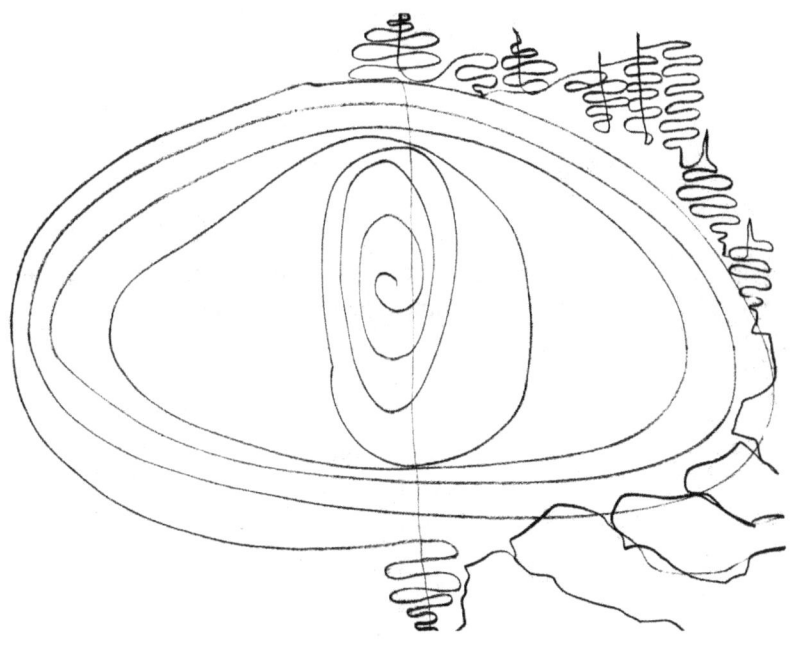

CREATIVE PRACTICE

Developing supportive tools

Start writing a simple list of the things that you enjoy, and that just make you feel good. Lists are good to have handy—they are especially supportive when we are tired . . . too weary to think clearly to the next step. Turning to such tools when times are tough or when you are feeling low or insecure can help to renew your energy and lift your mood.

The following is part of my support list. Create your own list under these headings:

Spiritual	**Mental**	**Physical**	**Sensual**	**Emotional**
Meditation	Study	Bike riding	Fresh air	Hugs
Chanting	Movies	Skiing	Sunshine	Playing with
Singing	Books	Dancing	Lovely	my children
Reading		Camping	clothes	A puppy
Support group			Time with my lover	
Long walks			Slow dancing	
Deep breathing				

Set up a blank chart with the above headings on a separate page. There is no right or wrong for where things are placed. Some activities overlap in various categories.

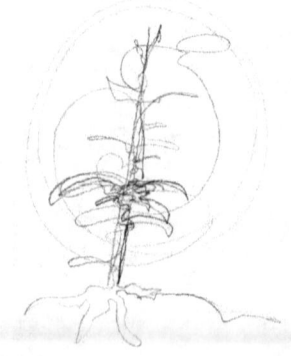

CREATIVE PRACTICE

Supportive chart

I designed this chart to include things I regularly do, as well as things I want more support on. Occasionally, I modify the chart. The more checks I have, the better I feel. Awarding myself checkmarks helps me to include more positive things in my life, and even to trim off a few pounds. For each chart I complete, I give myself a reward. Whenever I find myself getting worn down, tired, and feeling overwhelmed, then I know it's time to pull out this chart. It quickly lets me know what I've been neglecting. Below is my own example, but you can create your own categories.

Every day, "feed" all aspects of yourself, including your spiritual, emotional, mental, physical, and sensual aspects.

SUPPORTIVE CHART										
Morning stretch										
Breathing										
Journal writing										
Gratitude list										
A walk										
Other exercise										
Taking a rest										
Spiritual reading										
Humming, singing										
Sunshine										
Hugs										
Fun										
Less fat/fried stuff										
Healthy snacks, apples										
Smaller meat portions										
More veggies										
Evening stretch										

Enjoying self-esteem

Self-esteem is a realistic respect for yourself and includes awareness of your talents, abilities, and the goodness of your heart.

Being humble is
accepting and honouring your abilities.

Excel.

Excel at your work. Strive for excellence. Continue to expand your horizons. Experiment. Study. The growth of your style is an ongoing process. Follow your heart, and your style will grow and emerge. Keep moving and evolving. Some aspects may be daunting, but just remember that it is all part of the process. Don't give up! Create passion for yourself. It is your life.

Strut your stuff!

Follow your intuition. It's right.

UNDERSTANDING YOUR EMOTIONS

Do you ever get the feeling that there is something more you could be experiencing? That maybe there is something missing? Or maybe life just feels flat? Perhaps life lacks meaning or purpose. Somehow you feel unsettled . . . not quite right. It could be that you are unaware of your emotions, including the ones you've blocked. Perhaps you feel life is unmanageable.

Blocking the flow of emotions blocks avenues of creativity and passionate living. Blocking, suppressing, and/or holding emotions takes energy. It is tiring.

- Emotions can affect creativity in different ways.
- Emotions can inhibit and block creative flow.
- Emotions can enhance and inspire creativity.
- Emotions can provoke introspection and inspire opportunities.
- Blocked emotions may distort other emotions and attitudes.

Not understanding an emotion allows the emotion to take control, hijacking or paralyzing you. Understanding your emotions and moods can give you objectivity and the intelligence to remove yourself and think clearly about a situation. Then you can use those emotions to free up your creativity with confidence. With this awareness, you will be able to direct your emotional energy and let the creative energy flow through it.

To understand and communicate these sensations, you need to find a way to give them a "form" or "meaning."

Participation in the arts can do this. The arts can help to transcend an emotion or release blocked feelings. The arts provide a non-verbal vehicle for moving emotions that you might not otherwise be able to—or even want to—articulate.

Blocked emotions may distort other emotions and attitudes

Emotions that have been suppressed emerge eventually. Before then, they colour our attitude and affect how we respond.

***Suppressing feelings or emotions blocks us
from being open to all possibilities, being emotionally alive,
sensitive, and passionately living life to the fullest.***

A blocked emotion can show up exaggerated, defeated, and distorted somewhere else. Triggers that ignite us could be disguising some deeper unresolved emotion.

Note that "blocked emotion" does not mean being devoid of emotion. "Blocked emotion" could mean that the emotion is extreme, mutilated, distorted, and misdirected. For example, passionate lovemaking crosses a line and may actually be violent. Delirious celebrations that seem ecstatic could be rife with bingeing, hurtful jokes, and wild or self-destructive behaviour. How honest and clear are your emotions and reactions?

Emotions can block and inhibit creative flow

Anger, fear, or sadness can stop creativity in its tracks.

Anger can hinder creativity so much that it can blind and block any insight, because anger itself is so loud and dominating.

Fear of failing the class, fear of failing the teacher's expectations, fear of failing your own expectations and hopes could paralyze you and prevent you from even trying. Fear of looking foolish could stop any exploration or attempts.

Hopelessness or dread rooted in sadness or depression can dampen any energy needed to start a creative endeavour.

Anger

Unreleased anger consumes us and can hurt us physically and emotionally. Anger can reside in depression, disappointment, indignation, and frustration, feeling betrayed, annoyed, or fed up. Suppressed anger can ensnare creativity. It may appear as sarcasm, controlling random outbursts or careful perfectionism. Suppressed anger can result in feeling unworthy, tired, hurt, guilty, powerless, fearful, depressed, and even in denial of justified anger. Suppressed anger could also unleash a furious passion that could burn through any soul, and express itself in loud, staccato music, harsh lines and wild colour combinations.

How will you let your anger out? How will you guide your anger to be productive and to motivate you in an active, positive way? What opportunity has anger brought you? Is the anger justified in the current situation? For example, has someone hurt a child? Or is the anger a reaction to a story line or childhood societal lie?

Fear

How fearful are you? Fear can be obvious or not. How can fear be useful? It can be disguised as over-vigilance, over-analysis and/or over-protecting.

How do you know? What is the source?

Being careful, protective, and vigilant can be wise. Analyzing can be useful. But when do these behaviours become unbalanced? Are any of them stopping you from realizing your dreams and goals? Are they hurting you in some way by tiring you, stressing you, and perhaps draining you?

Sadness

Unreleased sadness often stagnates and gets thicker and heavier. Giving in to sadness does not mean that it will stay or stay long. Distracting yourself from sadness gives it licence to contaminate other thoughts. Facing your sadness and feeling it, rather than denying it, permits the sadness to be released in its own time. If your sadness could move, how would it move?

Guilt

The Tibetans do not have a word for "guilt." Guilt is more than feeling morally responsible. Guilt is usually a negative focus upon oneself, contributing to a lack of confidence and unworthiness. Guilt can make you feel over-responsible; it can lead you to overwork; it can immobilize you and make you sensitive to others' opinions of you. Guilt can be disguised as serving others first. Guilt can misguide you in your actions.

Is there anything useful in feeling guilty? Feelings of guilt can be so uncomfortable that you are motivated to change your whole approach to life.

Consider the responsibility of all parties and circumstances. Reflect on motivation and intention. Consider forgiving yourself. Is it reasonable to think that as a human you would never make mistakes? It is important to learn to forgive yourself.

Shame

Shame isn't commonly talked about. Often there is shame around *feeling* shame.

The feelings of shame are so painful they can lead to violence or suicide. Shame strikes the deepest at the heart. It is often an unbearable inner torment of humiliation, defeat, and alienation.

Where are the opportunities in shame? Healthy shame sets a framework for our humility—who we are and are not. Shame shows us our limits and sets our standards for right and wrong.

When shame takes over our identity as a belief that we are defective as a human being, it becomes toxic. This distorted form of shame is extremely harsh and harmful. Shame and guilt are rooted in fears, beliefs, and behaviours. Acting out of shame is not productive to healthy, joyful living. Consider the root causes of irrational beliefs, despair of the past, denial of past hurts, not letting go of the past, fear of rejection, victimization, silent withdrawal in anger, sense of powerlessness, sense of hopelessness, and lack of forgiveness of oneself.

Getting over shame is hard work. You'll need to do consistent work on yourself. It's best if you can get support—in therapy or from a very empathic friend.

Many people I work with worry that if they give in to an unpleasant emotion, they will remain in that state. No one can sustain any one emotion for a lengthy period of time. As humans, we fluctuate in the broad spectrum of emotions. The key is to manage unpleasant emotions so the pleasant ones can prevail.

In these harder emotions, consider their quality, intensity, and purpose.

Affirm yourself. You deserve a happy life. We all deserve a happy life.

Honest expressions

> **All our expressions are linked to our emotions,
> which can find expression as playfulness, creativity,
> hurtfulness, kindness, sadness, and anger.**

We need to be honest with ourselves, our reactions, and our responses in life. We need to know who we are. How do we get there? By experiencing our life. Throughout our lives we are becoming who we are. We need to be aware of ourselves, each other, and everything around us. To understand ourselves, we need to learn about who we are, the families and culture from which we come. In the understanding, it is possible to choose wisely what is best for us and our family.

At first, such conscious development of awareness and understanding of your own emotions may seem daunting and draining. Being fully with your emotions is not always easy or fun. But the result of your efforts will provide greater sensitivity, happiness, and satisfaction, as well as a profound sense of gratitude. You will still feel the not-so-pleasant emotions, but with recognition and understanding, they will seem short-lived and not as wounding as they used to be.

Whatever emotion you are experiencing, give it time to be felt in its entirety and time to be understood.

Emotions can enhance and inspire creativity

When you feel any of the debilitating emotions, try to express them in your journal. Paint your sadness, paint how you are feeling. Or write a short poem about how you are feeling. Alternatively, if you are sad, be quiet and let the emotion be. Invest your time in really feeling that emotion. If it would help, share with a friend. You may be surprised how the sadness, the fear, or the anger gives way to calm. Think how you can support yourself through such emotions. Will they stop you? Or will they drive you, motivate you?[4]

If you feel wistful when others revel in their creative aspiration, and sense that something is holding you back, consider whether you are experiencing an emotional block.

---

[4] Understanding and working with our emotions can be an ongoing challenge. Among the publications listed in the Resources section are several that offer insights and assistance with this process.

Some of the greatest love songs, operatic arias, plays, and movies have been written from the saddest hearts. "Fado" is a Portuguese folksong style filled with mournful lament.

Some emotions are so strong and passionate that they demand broad, bold brushstrokes and vibrant colours. Most people want to tell their story and want everyone to hear it in one creative form or another.

In my classes

When you draw or paint strokes, are they tight, careful, and controlled or wild and strong? Does your expression seem to have a mind of its own?

Terry agonized that he could not paint the way I did, even though he understood what I was showing him about values and shading. His strokes were strong, bold, and vertical. His colours shouted. He felt self-conscious. While Terry could draw and paint photo-realistically, it bored and constrained him. I encouraged him to listen to what his heart, his body, and his life experience had to say.

Who really knows where these urges come from? Do we need to know? Art is a safe way to express such urges freely.

Terry became freer with his painting and more comfortable with his strong strokes. His new-found confidence flowed over into other aspects of his life. Terry became more satisfied and content.

Another one of my students revels in fine detail. After a few years of studying with me, Sophia confessed that she trimmed one of her brushes because she could not find one small enough to make her tiny paint strokes. She was very self-conscious of painting slowly and taking lots of time to finish a piece. She felt she was falling behind because she was the slowest in the class. Hoping to speed herself up, Sophia was desperately taking classes that compelled boldness and daring materials. She even forced herself to use wide brushes.

Sophia had been taught that being slow meant you were not as intelligent as others. I assured her that in the arts, taking your time was a valuable goal and quality. I suggested that she sit quietly in her home studio and ponder on what she loved doing and how she felt, assuring her that she would find her answer by listening to herself. A few weeks later, Sophia joyfully noted that she was happiest when lost in minute detail. She loved it for itself and for no other reason. Now she follows her tiny strokes, and feels free to paint and explore in this way. Her artistic sensibility continues to express itself, and her paintings continue to evolve. And she is thrilled doing it.

Challenge yourself or stretch yourself creatively by exploring uncomfortable, awkward, or unfamiliar areas.

It is important to know that is what you are doing for growth. To agonize and to try to squeeze yourself into a role that does not fit you doesn't make sense. Life is a gift and far too short.

Emotions can give you an opening

Instead of hating, suppressing, or avoiding difficult emotions, consider their usefulness!

Consider an important benefit of strong emotions: spending time with them invites further introspection. Compassion and deep thought can cultivate storytelling, teaching, writing, and drama.

Reflecting on any emotion, whether it be anger, fear, sadness, joy, compassion, or love, can inspire deep thoughtfulness and creative expression in various forms. In turn, the creative acts that emerge from introspection can result in heightened creativity, more balance, and satisfaction.

Passionate feelings make me feel very much alive.

What is joy?

Joy, oh joy, sheer glee!

Are you happy? What is your inner dance like?

What does that really mean?

Happiness has different levels. It could be mild satisfaction or a profound feeling of well-being. It could be effervescent, light and bubbly, or wildly jubilant. Many aspects of our lives, such as possessions, a partner, children, friends, positions, accomplishments, and busyness bring different levels of happiness. These aspects are mainly outside of ourselves, but can affect us internally.

> **There is also a deep, inner calm that is solid and long-lasting.**
>
> **Such happiness is unshakable because it is deeply rooted in our being.**
>
> **Outside forces and elements cannot break it apart.**

This inner core of happiness permeates and affects all that is around us. Even through adversity, this deep happiness carries with it a strong core of resilience, an appreciation of our life and our senses. It brings hope and calm and can cushion us from total despair and hopelessness.

> **Deep happiness emerges from being authentic to yourself.**

This includes a strong spiritual foundation. It is not a superficial masking of other emotions or negatives. Authentic feelings still flow—up and down, as in sadness, worry, frustration, fear, anger, joy, passion, and excitement. Even though some moments may not feel that pleasant, we can still explore their usefulness. We are still able to experience deep appreciation of our gift, the miracle of life. How will we contribute to one another? It is the same miracle with its tapestry of feelings.

Is it your goal to be authentic, honest, and approachable and to gain a sense of power and ownership at the same time? Permit yourself to feel emotions honestly and to be clear where those feelings belong. Are they part of your emotional history or someone else's? By acting authentically, you set an example that will help others to be authentic, too. Such clarity cultivates an inner calm, which leads to harmony within the community and contributes to peace around us.

Happily centred people celebrate each other's successes and happiness. Deep joy is cultivated when you are centred and fully present in your life.

How do you cultivate this deeper happiness? By living with acute awareness of who you are and who you are becoming. Truly understanding yourself embraces spiritual, mental, emotional, physical, and sensual awareness. It is a continuing lifelong journey.

> ***Deep joy flows when all aspects of your life flow. Deep joy flows in all aspects of surrender, uncertainty, forgiveness, and appreciation.***

CREATIVE PRACTICE

Exploring emotion

Try really feeling the emotion and being with it. Then try to recognize it.

Take some long, deep breaths.

Then try to create some space between feeling that emotion and feeling a response to it, for now—not questioning it.

Take as much time as you need to work out what you are thinking. This might be a good time to record your thoughts in a journal or perhaps share them with an objective listener.

Does your thinking feel reactive? Are these old thoughts, old memories?

Are the thoughts a pattern? Are they repetitive?

Are your thoughts really someone else's expectations?

What is the source of your emerging thoughts about the emotion?

Do you know what the triggers for this emotion are? What triggers these emotions?

Is your response something that you will be happy with?

Is it productive?

Will your response achieve what you really want?

Sometimes it seems that any choice you make will produce an undesirable outcome. Then you need to pick the action that is least undesirable.

You have choices about how you respond to situations and emotions. And know that your choices will definitely affect the outcome.

Sometimes,

it is beneficial to pause.

Wait a day or night or longer before taking action.

What about love?

Love has probably been written about more than any other subject.

Is it infinite benevolence or good will? Is it sexual? Is it generous? Sensitive? Is love complicated? Simple?

There is a complete goodness about feeling love.

What is love in its purest form?

Love just is.

Love cannot be love with negative emotions. When there is fear and pain, love is pushed aside.

We complicate love with expectations and desires.

Love is to be and to give, rather than to acquire.

When we can live with love in a pure way, it is natural and nurturing. Love can flow in and out of us, in our thoughts and our actions. Living with love permeates everything around with it.

Looking at yourself and your life through eyes of pure love can open doors of joy and bliss that you never dreamed existed.

Loving another person or a cause can give one value and purpose. With this value and purpose we can endure anything.

I Come from Love

I come from love,
at first or at last.

I come from tired ways
that once were fresh.

I come from many mothers,
once daughters too.

I come from fear,
at last or at first.

I come from energy
inside and out.

I come from you
and you from me.

I come from the cool dirt
of the earth.

I come from the air's
hollow sky.

I come from the water
licking my lips.

I come from spirit
breathlessly clear.

Somewhere in my body,
my memory is perfect.

My journey
is mine to remember.

chapter five

CREATIVITY LOOKS LIKE THIS

Creative people share a deeply held belief
that they are creative.
In believing that you are creative, you are
opening yourself to play with possibilities.

Begin your thoughts prepared for flexibility.

Be gentle with yourself.
Go slowly and take small steps.

In time, you will leap and fly.

Your desires will be fulfilled
more than you have imagined.

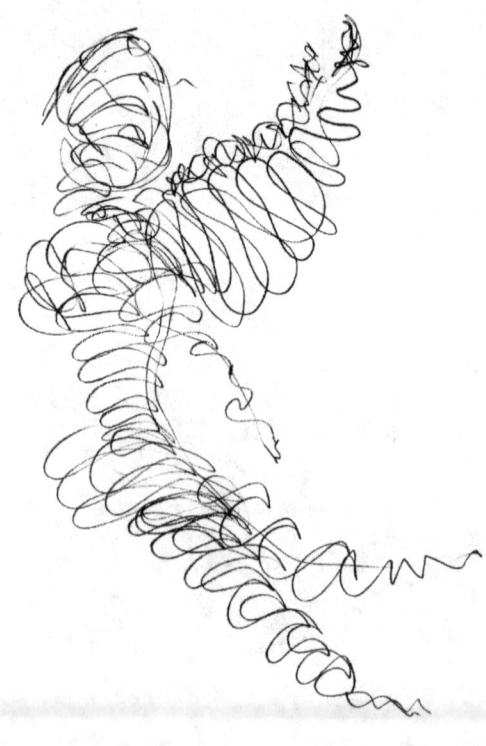

BEING CREATIVE

What is it to be a creative person?

Being creative implies a deep awareness of yourself, including your reactions, thoughts, and feelings, your body and its functions, as well as your spirituality. It is an awareness that flows outward toward all that is around you and in everything that you do.

"Creativeness" implies and encompasses inquisitiveness and learning, as well as openness to any and all possibilities.

Being creative is more than just surviving our daily world and its challenges. Creativity involves the ability to embrace change as opportunity, to recognize the opportunities inherent in problems, and to have fun with happy abandon.

Being creative is taking the time to see beyond the ordinary, often bringing something new into existence—an invention, a discovery, or a process. This applies not only to the arts, but also to every aspect of daily life, including relationships, work, and leisure activities.

The creative thinker tackles questions and obstacles with the mindset of an explorer, eager to see all possibilities, to discover multiple choices. We want to be creative so that we will have wisdom in our choices. Any and all questions are valid. Always. Asking questions is another part of exploration. Questions and answers can lead to other questions and answers. We do not know where a question will take us, so it is important to ask regardless. We cannot prejudge the quality of the question or the final answers. Otherwise, we are blocking possibilities and development.

Be curious.

Be inquisitive.

Creativity is nature's gift, a part of our humanity
to exploit and to revel in throughout our life journey.
It is our creativity that spurs curiosity and growth.
It is our creativity that sparks our imagination
on the life journey of exploration and discovery.

You can learn to stimulate creativity in every aspect of your life. To do so takes awareness, reflection, and the desire to expand all that you know and do.

What is creative mindfulness?

Mindfulness involves being "in the moment" by opening all your senses, by deliberate awareness of details all around you—shapes, sounds, smells, movements, everything.

This entails a deliberate and watchful slowing down to absorb what you are sensing. These details can become the "files" for your creativity, and include:

- Making the effort to understand and appreciate the wisdom of what is true and valuable
- Asking questions to learn rather than to evaluate
- Thinking non-judgmentally
- Realizing that our battles are inside us, not outside
- Opening your mind deliberately to what is different
- Adopting a "beginner's mind," as if you know nothing
- Appreciating stillness, reflection, and meditation
- Connecting to your spirituality

Thinking creatively

Creative thinking involves more than just thinking about colours and art, notes and music, words and poems, acting and drama.

- Sometimes it involves thinking like a critic—pensive, analytical, judgmental, and appraising.
- Sometimes it is thinking passionately, wildly, and unedited.
- Sometimes it is thinking like a child—playful, curious, and without preconceived notions.
- Sometimes it is strongly focused on achieving a dream.

Creative thinking uses all modes of thinking: verbal and non-verbal, analytical, symbolic, abstract, concrete, temporal, rational, digital, linear, spatial, analogical, intuitive, and holistic. Creative thinking switches tracks easily as required.

My students comment frequently on how learning artistic skills has helped their creative thinking to flourish in all aspects of their lives. Their attitudes change, their awareness is heightened, and even their math and reading skills advance. Emotionally and spiritually, they evolve.

Creativity is not exclusive to any one person. It is only elusive to those believing that they are not creative or artistic. Telling yourself that you are not creative effectively blocks your own creative flow.

> **Believe that you are creative and you will be.**

Try it and see.

Creativity is born from daydreaming, imagining, visualizing, and just plain being curious and inventive. Do you allow time for daydreaming, for imagination and for invention? Do you unknowingly squelch your own creativity and ingenuity, as well as your children's, by spending a disproportionate amount of time with mass-produced toys, games, and TV viewing? How do you judge creativity?

Want to be more creative?

Allow creative thinking time a special slot in each day and keep reading.

RESISTING CREATIVITY

I am an artist, yet I often assume that what I am creating is wrong or just not working out. I frequently have to reassure myself that what I am creating *is* right and *is* working out.

Self-deprecation and insecurity hit everyone.

Recognize such thoughts, push them aside, and move on. The point of creativity is to try out—in your imagination, if not in fact—all kinds of possibilities. Then make the leap and do what excites you.

Remember that even as you are exploring, learning, and developing, you are gaining in the quest to reach your full potential.

> *Part of being creative*
> *is the exciting process of becoming*
> *what and who you uniquely are.*
> *Enjoy the process!*

Reading about creativity is not a substitute for involving yourself in creative activities.

While daydreaming, you frequently think in words and images. So why do you resist expressing this free thinking in painting, sculpture, poetry, music, or song? Not to explore your hesitation to "let go" is to deprive yourself of the fullness of creative experience that could be yours.

Take time to daydream, imagine, and visualize. Imagery permits safe visual exploration and fantasizing without boundaries. Anything is possible, all dreams come true, and there are no restrictions or conditions. Dream up questions and seek answers that are different and new. Learning to visualize enhances human experience even as it expands and strengthens your thinking process, your ability to solve problems, and your living skills. All that is required is fearless practice. Set your creativity free! Dare to imagine the ridiculous!

Imagery in the form of dreaming and visualizing is all too often considered distracting in our educational system. Generally, we discourage and sometimes dismiss dreaming and visual thinking. My experience as a student and teacher is that most people do not make time for this.

Fearful resistance to exploring creative ventures appears in many guises: for example, feeling suddenly tired or hungry, getting a headache, getting fidgety and feeling nervous—or procrastinating. Be aware of such feelings in yourself or in others and be gentle.

As confidence emerges, these "symptoms" will dissipate and creativity will continue.

STIMULATING YOUR CREATIVE ENERGY

You can find ways to create a mood that invites creativity to flow. You are the master of your brain. Learn how to seductively squeeze those creative juices.

Set a relaxed, harmonious mood

Go for a walk, do yoga or tai chi, meditate, visualize, listen to calming tapes, chant, and definitely include deep breathing. Sit on the grass and watch a tree grow. Choose the best time for you and permit whatever works to calm your heart and mind.

Clean out the cobwebs

Journalling is fantastic housecleaning for those extra words and repetitive sentences flying around your head. Just write whatever comes into your head, even if it's "I don't know what to write," or, "I feel silly," or, "I have to meet this client," or, "I have to get this out of the freezer soon," and so forth. Don't judge what you write or how often you think it. Just write it.

Journal

Use your journal to record dreams, quick ideas, and even blurry visions. Your journal can be thought of as a vacuum cleaner, sucking up the words in your mind just like dust—except that, if you want to go back and read the words, they'll be there. And, like housecleaning, the more consistently you do it, the less daunting it becomes.

Rearrange a few things

Change the colour of some of your accessories. Turn things around, upside-down or inside-out. By physically changing the look of your surroundings, you stimulate your brain to think along different pathways.

Check out your workspace

Create a mood with colour, lighting, posters, pictures, support materials, quotes, and fun things that make you smile. What does your workspace say to you? Look at it as if you were visiting. How would you evaluate it? Is it an inspirational place to be?

Try music

Gear yourself up and create an energetic flow by listening to some zany beat music. Keep a collection of music that inspires you, that makes you groove. Find music that gets you moving. Dance to it, draw to it, run to it, write to it.

STIMULATING YOUR SENSES

You already know that humans have five senses: taste, touch, smell, hearing, and seeing, as well as a sixth sense called intuition. Applying creative mindfulness can enhance each of these senses. That is, slow down to place yourself fully within the details of each experience at the moment it occurs.

Touch something new

Touch something that you usually do not touch. Caress the milk jug . . . or eggs before you crack them. Close your eyes while you caress. Describe to yourself what you are feeling physically and emotionally. Touch an appliance, a bouquet of flowers, the telephone, a chair, a pencil, Jell-O, and describe the sensations to yourself. How would you paint the texture?

Try a new taste

Explore a different type of kiss or lick. Taste all the hot seasonings and different sweeteners; compare berry flavours. Search out something with texture. Note how different textures evoke different tastes and sensations.

Listen to unfamiliar music and sounds

What are you hearing? Turn everything off in your house. Now what are you hearing? Sing. If you do sing, try singing something totally different. Listen to the sound of your car; listen to the sound of the bus or the train.

Smell something unfamiliar

Treat your nose to a garden, to essential oils, or to a delightful barbeque. Slice a lemon, burn some toast, smell your soap. Smell a rock.

Stare at something as if for the first time

Study blades of grass. Roll over, look up at the trees, and follow their patterns against the sky. Then come inside and notice how many colours reflect off any surface. Look at water—what colour is it, really? Or are you seeing the reflection in the water?

Pay attention to your intuition. Stimulating your senses revitalizes your spirits and increases your energy. Stimulating your senses in new ways stimulates your brain in new ways.

Leonardo Da Vinci — Italian painter, sculptor, engineer, musician, mathematician, and scientist — knew how to stimulate, heighten, and constantly caress his senses. He knew how to live well and fully. He knew how to keep the sparkle in his life and in his eyes. His happiness just to be alive was expressed in his vibrant creativity.

He made time to ponder quietly and alone.

He luxuriated in clothes of the finest silks and velvets that flowed and caressed his body when he walked.

He hired musicians to play for him while he painted.

He ate the finest foods and exercised his body.

He delighted in scented oils that aroused his sense of smell.

He stimulated his brain with puzzles and he never stopped learning.

CHANGING YOUR CHANNELS

If I come into my studio after a breakfast grumbling match with my family, the emotional residue could block my creativity. Any feeling or state of being that keeps you from being creative is a block. Feeling hurried or distracted with worry, feeling tired or feeling guilty for taking the time, feeling insecure, afraid of not producing enough, or even wanting to produce a certain result—all hamper that creative flow. Internal and external factors affect how you function.

After thirty years of artistic endeavours, over time and with practice, I have learned to listen to my inner voice, even when it says to take a walk or chant in the midst of "the fifty-item list of things to do." I used to resist. I'm not sure why. Sometimes I'd drag myself to my place of slowing down, and with a big sigh, I would do it. And each time, the investment paid off. In the process of slowing down, I move in sync with my world again. I think more clearly and move ahead with increased confidence.

When I am tense, overwhelmed, or overcome with emotion, I am too blind to see where I am and I cannot hear my inner voice.

That is when life becomes a bigger mess, and I drop things and forget things, I backtrack and feel dissatisfied. These days, I don't go too far without seeing what is happening. I have learned to recognize my signals, wryly smile at myself, and attempt to take care of myself and the situation as soon as possible.

Sometimes, just showing up at the page, paper, canvas, or on the dance floor and starting something will initiate the flow of creativity. It may feel stilted, forced, or haphazard for a while until you get warmed up. Eventually, the creative juices start flowing.

As you try certain ways to draw yourself into creative concentration, you will find what works best. Just go with what feels right for you. As you slow down, your inner voice becomes clearer.

- Listen to yourself.
- Explore new frontiers.
- Take the time to practise.
- Explore a new skill or hobby that has no relationship to what you already do.
- Try something you never thought you could do.

chapter six

THE ARTS EXPERIENCE

True freedom in art is when
we have no judgments or expectations
and we do art for no reason
except for the experience.

EXPERIENCING ART

In this chapter, I refer to visual arts: drawing and painting. At other times, more explanation has been added to further enhance the expressive arts experience.

What is art?

Is it a communication between the maker and community?

Is it a reflection of a culture?

Is it a connection between the maker and nature?

Or is it just an idea or reaction expressed?

In the never-ending debate to define art, there is agreement that the artistic expression, in whatever form, is about life and is a form of communication. In appreciating this, we connect with the maker and often more deeply with a part of ourselves.

Why should you consider becoming involved in a creative art process?

> *Experiencing art — in any form — builds a solid foundation for the skills of living.*

In the act of artistic expression, we experience an evolution of tolerance, self-discipline, critical thinking, and creativity. The art process is experiential. Art is tangibly honest and real. Becoming personally involved in any aspect of the arts has deep and long-lasting effects.

Art is all around us. There is art in painting, music, dance, mathematics, science, nature, living, and playing. All are connected, because all encompass the imaginative creativity of arranging elements into a composition that affects both the doer and the viewer, expanding our understanding and appreciation.

Just experiencing the process of creating art can be enough for the doer. So much occurs within that artful process. The arts stimulate our senses, in turn stimulating our perspective.

> *Art makes our life rich.*

A natural human response = creativity = arts

In every culture, using pencil and paper or sticks in the sand, children draw pictures of their environment. In every culture, children drum and dance. Children copy sounds, play complementary rhythms, and compose sound landscapes. They find many ways to mimic all that is important in their environment—the central people in their lives, their homes, animals, their surroundings, and their expressions. Children's play will often evolve into dance movement as they experiment with experiences.

> **Drawing, drumming, singing, and dancing can convey emotions—joy, sadness, mystification or confusion, passion or anger—where verbal articulation sometimes falters. The creativity of participation in the arts transcends emotion and communicates artful expression that requires no analysis or defence.**

Art just is. Art becomes, evolves, and often transforms the doer and the observer. The arts represent non-verbal forms of human communication, just as speech is our verbal form.

Developing whole-brain learning skills (logical and creative) in adults and children helps to develop a balance between verbal and non-verbal communication, rational or symbolic thinking, and stimulates temporal or intuitive thoughts.

Practising art involves heightening your perception of edges, spaces, relationships, and light and shadow, as well as perspective, rhythm, and contrast. It involves stretching all your senses to appreciate the smallest detail and the broadest scene. The ability to transcribe, decode, and compose parts into a unified, aesthetic whole represents the expression of observations filtered through individual senses that eventually result in original creativity in any form of the arts. While each person has these innate abilities, practising the arts—giving these abilities expression—enhances them.

Learning the basics—reading, writing, and math—is not enough. The boundaries of human knowledge are expanding at a rate that is impossible to keep pace with. To succeed personally and professionally in an ever-changing world, people need to develop the higher skills of creativity, such as problem-solving, communicating in different ways, self-discipline, tolerance, and critical thinking.

> *One of the most important gifts*
> *we can give our children is confidence in*
> *their ability to learn, think, and be creative.*

My experience working with corporations, institutions, and businesses to develop and enhance creativity in their employees has helped me to see that we are all looking for the same attributes: wisdom, abstract thinking, effective problem-solving, ingenuity, vitality, awareness, enthusiasm, and a passion for what we do.

> *Enhancing creative elements within life skills*
> *by encouraging participation in the arts*
> *is as good for business as it is for*
> *day-to-day living and well-being.*

There is a growing body of research and years of proven programs that support the power of the arts in the development of life skills and healing. Integrating the arts in any learning process increases the brain's ability to access and process other information more imaginatively than ever before.

The arts stimulate the brain in new and different ways.

Art is the voice in your heart

You may think you don't know enough about art. Well, I say that you do.

You know whether you like a piece of art, and that's enough, whether or not you respond to it.

I present the following exercise in my art classes and seminars: I hold up pieces of art in several styles and from different historical periods. The group is allowed three responses: "I like it," "I don't like it," and "Ho hum." Each art piece receives a mixed response. Regarding any piece of art, I have yet to receive unanimous agreement from any group. We have different tastes in food, colours, styles, haircuts, and partners—so why not different tastes in art?

People set trends. Some feel qualified to berate or to praise art. A trained eye can perhaps articulate some reasons for an opinion. Others are driven by approval and power. What one likes in raw passion, another enjoys in infinite detail. What fascinates one bores another. A piece, whether abstract, impressionistic, or realistic, may captivate your heart or it may motivate or even infuriate you.

Art can be a matter of taste and opinion.

Take a look at a few of our public art collections. You will find pieces that bore you, inspire you, anger you, or even excite you for different reasons. Your friends, family, and colleagues will likely all have different opinions.

Art is the voice of our hearts. Each voice resonates in a different way.

How can we attack the voice within us? How can we doubt it, when it alone is the only truth to our very nature at the time? Taking the time to study a piece of art and then to question or challenge it is different from simply denouncing the artist or the work. The study could provide the viewer with new understanding.

Each voice is important and has value. Each voice is expressed through individual experience. Each expression represents a voice that is on its own journey.

VENTURING INTO ART

I started art because I wanted to play. Today, it is still play, and more. It has opened up my life.

For me, posing nude is easier than showing someone my paintings, drawings, or poetry, which come from the depths of my soul, my deepest longings, vulnerable feelings, and passions—all raw and honest. Each painting is a part of me. It exposes me. Any foibles or inner weaknesses play havoc with my psyche. Maybe I pursue my development in art to search out any black hole that is trying to suck the fun out of my life, because sometimes the pursuit feels like a tormenting desire, a thirst that is never quenched. Yet, these feelings are also addictive and intoxicating. For me, art is an intimate dance with my life that keeps getting deeper and more passionate. As much as art exposes and chases deep, dark, secret blocks, it also enraptures me in a love and healing that has no words.

Art is also my "fix." If I didn't have my art, I am sure I would be dead, drunk, or drugged. At least my therapist thought so, and I think he may be right. Obviously, I am not dead, and I do not drink or indulge in recreational or pharmaceutical drugs. My addiction is art.

Art is my passion, my intimate craving. It is the water that quenches my thirst. Art is my silent healing. It helps to balance my unbalanced world. Art is my private partner and my hero. It leads me to explore other possibilities in my life. Art teaches me compassion and differing points of view. It opens me to meditation and gives me hope and peace of mind.

As a youth, I was fanatical about engaging in intense and long hours of solitary physical exercise. That added fuel to my fire and helped me survive, but I remained puzzled about any kind of inner resolve. An early drama class and a creative writing class helped to plant some creative perspective within my turmoil. They were the launching point that sent me off on other artistic endeavours.

Art gets my inspirational juices flowing. I see life differently through art and I am excited. My troubles get lost in art and my mind is always eased.

And I want more of it. Art is always there when I am ready to show up. The paper or canvas waits patiently for my brush strokes. They don't try to fix me, or change me, or push me to any conclusion. The brush strokes don't complain about the velocity of the sweep. Colours aren't critical or hurt by my choices or moods. Hundreds of canvases support my outpouring of emotional vigour without tiring. The dance floor holds me. The drum offers its rumble to me.

I did not always understand or recognize that this was my journey. I only noted emerging peace of mind and the joy I had in the play. Slowly, over time, and after hundreds of hours lost in my paintings, my memories and emotions became transformed and transcended. As I grew, I included other support tools for my well-being, such as breathing, chanting, exercise, soundscaping, dancing, eating well, thinking well, reading well, and simply living in the present.

As I became stronger and more aware, I also grew more in harmony with my life. My past now exists only as a dull roar, recognizable and manageable. The chaos of life continues to throw illusory curves and ruffle my exterior, but my support system is firm and strong.

Art is fun. If I am in the middle of what appears to be adversity, I now know it must be time to paint or to dance. I still take care of business, but including art means including a deep awareness and appreciation of myself. It softens the day's "yucky stuff" and simply brings me back to my miraculous life.

My promise to myself is always to include art in my day.

> **When you make a promise to yourself, be true to your desires. Remember to be gentle with yourself. Be aware of your expectations and differences as you explore your artistic endeavours.**

ART PROVOKES BENEFICIAL CHANGE

I am continually amazed by the changes that occur, as a person progresses through an art workshop, with language, inquisitiveness, self-confidence, and general abilities. In both adults and children, I have encountered a strong emotional change that evolved from being judgmental, reactionary, and stressed, toward an open, happy curiosity and willingness to look at an issue from differing points of view.

Benefits of personal involvement in art

- Problems seem to dissipate.
- Concerns and issues seem to find easier resolution.
- Life becomes quieter and more focused.
- Greater enthusiasm for life develops.
- Writing skills soar.
- Concentration and the ability to focus increase.
- Enhanced understanding and empathy for oneself, others, and our environment develops.
- Reading skills improve.
- Confidence and enthusiasm for learning increase.
- Higher self-esteem and happiness are expressed.
- Increased hope and confidence in our future with a global view emerge.

Art activity provides an intimate connection with our innate human nature.

Loving Your Life

Wounded at a young age

I have met people of all ages who have been wounded at various times in their lives. Some have abandoned art altogether, feeling suppressed, crushed, hurt, and inferior. Some were numb to the fact that their artistic selves had been squashed because early in their lives they accepted a suggestion that someone else was born with the "gift" of art.

Others still have a burning desire to try—to paint, to play music, to act, or to write. They want to try but are afraid because of some past horror story that diminished their confidence to learn and to develop artistic skills. The lucky ones find caring teachers who guide them past old blocks and help them to grow.

Ask yourself how you reacted the last time you abandoned an artistic endeavour. What were you thinking? Did you justify your action by belittling the process or dismissing the materials as cheap, the work as hasty or unimportant? Take another look at what prompted your action of rejection. Was it a comment, an inner voice, or someone's disparaging glance?

As you embark on your creative journey, it is important to put any unhappy memories behind you and to surround yourself with strong, healthy, supportive systems. While sensitivity is individual, each person requires nurturing.

Give yourself another chance.

SEEING LIFE DIFFERENTLY

As the arts stimulate the senses in different ways, we cannot help but see our lives differently.

As drawing helps us to see in a different way, sound play helps us to listen and hear differently.

The arts enliven the senses. Poking, tickling, spiking, soothing, with sound, colour, texture, taste, and smell.

As you explore and sensitize with your senses, you become more aware of yourself and your surroundings.

Your brain gets stimulated in different ways, opening up new thinking pathways.

All this is re-energizing, rejuvenating, and exciting.

Once again, you'll feel hopeful and stronger. It'll be easier to set up more support systems for yourself.

Life will feel more fun, less frustrating, less strained. You will feel more joy.

Everyone is creative.

Everyone has an innate ability to express that creativity in countless ways.

You are creative and you do have the ability to be artistic.

Right now, your creative perception, given the encouragement and opportunity for expression, would surprise you.

COMMON MISCONCEPTIONS ABOUT ART

Artistic talent is inherent, rare, and cannot be taught

"Talent" is natural ability usually expressed in a specialized area. Our desire and devotion affect our ability to do anything we set our minds to. With our passion, we can develop our learned ability into a talent. Many educators, parents, and students may not value artistic ability, especially with regard to potential employment. Yet, who does not value creative, innovative, resilient thinking in everyday life?

A "talented" artist draws from memory and imagination

Many artists research their subjects, collect pictures, use photographs for reference, and prepare study sketches to create pictures. I often hear a gasp when I show students how to use tools of the trade, such as viewfinders, graphs, and references. "But that's cheating," someone will say. Do we sometimes feel that way because these tools make the task easier?

One should discover artistic ability only through experimentation

When I owned an art shop, people often came in and sighed with envy at the displayed art, confiding that they had tried to paint and draw but without success. After some discussion, I invariably learned that their materials were inferior and the instruction incomplete. Painting with cheap materials is like trying to slice a tomato with a dull knife. Ability may be discovered through experimentation, but it is enhanced with care, knowledge, perseverance, and encouragement.

Art has no practical use and is mindless play

Art is big, passionate, and a profoundly personal expression that forms a major part of our communication, whether artistic or therapeutic. Art can express what words cannot. Art is one piece of the puzzle that can help make sense of the world around us. Can you imagine a world without music, dance, architecture, design, colour, and paintings?

Abstraction is messy and not real art

Art has many purposes. Art can communicate basic feelings through shape, line, and colour. Abstract art can explore and experiment where realism might not. Abstract art can be healing, playful, and provocative, and it can transcend commonly held beliefs. While abstract art might not always be appealing, it can have a raw honesty, and can reveal extraordinary significance, magnifying ordinary things and forcing viewers to see differently, thus enhancing their powers of observation and evoking powerful emotions.

Many abstract artists can paint realistically, but prefer to express themselves more spontaneously.

Expressive art accesses the bodily sensations, although they can be accompanied by, or used to express, some sort of idea or plan.

With no boundaries and no need to mirror reality, abstract art is especially approachable for new artists. As an artist, you can just enjoy the process for the sake of it. Many of my students start with abstract art and enjoy playing so much that they later pursue foundational and other traditional art classes.

Only beginners fear the white page

That stark, blank page staring back at you is daunting, whether you are a beginner or a practising artist. I have been painting for over thirty years, and each fresh piece of paper is intimidating. The bigger the canvas, the louder the intimidation. My fellow artists experience similar anxieties. How to begin? Do I just leap in? What first? What if? Expectations can blunt that creative flow, and the initial fear never goes completely away. Instead, you can learn to accept it as part of the creative process, and eventually learn how to abate it. There are many exercises and warm-ups to soften and abolish this beginning fear. I use the connected line exercise explained on page 178.

Artists are always pleased with their work

Rarely is there a piece that totally satisfies the creator's inner critic. Drawing, painting, music, acting, dancing, and writing all require practice and patience. Our desires and intellects are always a step ahead of our practical skill level, leaving us constantly critical and disappointed. Skills are developed through time and dedication. The process of art—like any type of creativity—is one of exploration and increasing development of skill and ideas. It is a process constantly shifting and evolving.

PREPARING FOR YOUR ARTISTIC JOURNEY

Art requires an exploration and development of skill and ideas. Be gentle with yourself. Leave your inner critic behind. Remember, this is your artistic journey—just for yourself.

Drawing can be learned

Many of us think we can't draw because we draw like a child. The reason some of us still draw like a six- or eight-year-old is because that is generally when development of our drawing skills stopped.

Learning to draw is just as much a matter of development and practice as is solving math equations, tying our shoes, riding a bicycle, or driving a car.

Drawing is a skill that can be taught and learned. It is simple, natural, and fun.

When you learn how to draw, you learn how to see.

As you learn how to observe and to really see, you are learning perception skills. You will rediscover your own world through drawing.

Often students come back after a drawing class remarking how they hadn't noticed that the road home was pink, or that clouds have very little white in them. In drawing, you will be observing with care, focusing intently, and gaining a growing fascination with everyday things. Working through aspects of drawing, you will see how objects and colours change when viewed from different perspectives.

You will never look at a common object in the same way again.

Drawing is a good way to begin your artistic journey and is a foundational skill that can be applied to other arts and to any aspect of life because it enhances perception, observation, concentration, and coordination. Drawing is approachable and practical, as it requires very few materials and little expense.

If you feel uncomfortable about signing up for a class, trust your instincts and explore the reasons. Find out about different courses and class options, and listen to students' comments about their teachers. Like a beginning student in any course of study, you need and deserve nurturing and a solid support system to develop a strong foundation of knowledge and confidence in your ability. Not every teacher or class is a fit.

Browsing the countless art books available and practising with a variety of art materials will be helpful, but they might not address individual needs and questions. Experienced artists with teaching ability can offer individual support and provide resources. The classroom setting also encourages students to get in touch with each other. The level of ability attainable is up to you—your sensitivity, your passion and devotion, your life experiences, and, of course, the time you invest in practising your technique.

From my teaching experience, I would recommend beginners' drawing courses of ten to twelve weeks (twenty-five to thirty hours). This length and time frame will help beginners to establish a solid foundation that they can build on in their journey, including the development of perception skills and the opportunity to practise new-found skills. Such courses are also a fundamental way for students to get in touch with other students and resources and establish a supportive network.

Warm-up drawings and study drawings are a way of downloading vital details about your subject. This practice provides you with information for future drawings. Everything you absorb must come out somehow. It is the addition of your imagination, interpretation, and style that will make your drawing uniquely yours, even though inspiration may have come from many sources.

Preparing for your expressive art journey

Expressive arts can be different than practising and developing an art form.

In practising and developing an art form, you learn foundational skills and structure for that particular discipline. The practice is focusing on developing material and hand/eye coordination skills. For instance, in drawing, the focus is getting familiar with materials, lines, lighting, position, and composition; or in music, its tone, notes, and rhythm.

Expressive arts can be much simpler and purer. It can be learning an art form, or simply banging or pounding a drum to express a feeling or situation.

Expressive arts is about responding with an urge that may not have descriptive words.

And yes, it is possible to mix foundation art disciplines with this purer expression. How you manage it is really your creation.

Art provides a place for risk-taking

Often, we cannot articulate our feelings or even understand them. Sometimes, words are not enough. We might not want to risk exploring these feelings or even know how to explore them. Art can be a safe and gentle way to process feelings or issues. We know that as soon as a feeling is acknowledged, whether verbally or non-verbally, it is somehow transformed and can serve, instead of hinder, our progress.

Working in the arts is a safe way to transform and articulate our feelings and at the same time develop life skills.

Exploring art can take different paths. As you evolve in your art, you may choose structure and technique, or you may seek deeper understanding of a particular medium or a balance in harmony and design. Involvement in the arts could help you to find and express a flow and calmness within yourself. Perhaps you will expose and cleanse your rage. Perhaps you want to jar, shock, or wake up through your art. Perhaps you really don't know where you are. Finding your place in practising art could help you to find your way.

What does art require?

Engaging in any artistic pursuit requires risk and passion. And that risk and passion is deserving of quality equipment, materials, and care. Your process is worthy of consideration. Celebrate your expression of art. It, too, is worthwhile.

Find the process, the tools, and the zone that works for you. These will excite your creative passion into delirious fever. Oh yes, you will be hot!

But how can anyone frolic in a delightful party of inspirations with tools that hack, skip, or hesitate?

If your tools and materials are awkward and give you grief, how can they continue to fuel your creative juices? Where will you get the energy to leap with your artistic endeavours?

High-quality tools and materials produce the best art and will continually expand your ability to express yourself. The experience of art becomes ecstatic. Proper tools and materials are intoxicating. My spirit revels in rich, thick, juicy, vibrant colours. Mysterious and captivating textures lure me into their secrets. Using brushes that dance with me while painting arouses my senses, excites me, and fills me with energy. Enjoy the sensuous and often unpredictable movement of the paint itself. Be open to experiment. Quality tools are a privilege and gift to be enjoyed and revelled in.

Discover your "comfort zone" for visual arts

Did you know that we each have an optimum working surface area where we do our best work? This is where our strokes are even, can be placed where we want them, and end up being the intended shape.

The size of the zone could be about 15 cm by 15 cm (6 inches by 6 inches) to about 30 cm by 30 cm (12 inches by 12 inches) while seated, or much larger while standing.

Have you ever noticed when writing a letter that the effort to write gets strained near the edge of the page, and the script becomes slanted or sloppy? Each person's working zone differs. It could be in front of your body centre or a little to the right or left, up or down, slightly this way or that. You may prefer to work on a flat surface or on a slanted easel.

Working on larger surfaces, you might note that the quality of your work changes when you are outside your zone, so you would need to adjust the surface position to make your work more manageable. Your optimum area will feel comfortable, and the intended strokes or motions will come with ease.

Discover your optimum working zone by experimenting with different locations. Try standing or sitting, try working on a table, on the floor, at a light table, or with an easel. When you find your comfort zone, you can adjust your work so it is always in your zone.

It will feel right.

What to paint?

> *Paint what is in your heart. React, respond, relate, and commiserate with yourself. Allow your relationship with yourself and your surroundings to merge and emerge within the medium.*

What excites you? What torments you?

You can be stuck in the structural part of learning about art and forget what is in your heart—the ethereal part. What makes your soul sing? What makes your soul cry? What challenges you? What mysteries do you desire to unfold?

In the studio the other day, a student studying my painting said, "You're not afraid to try anything." The watercolour painting was full of strong strokes, bold, rich colours, crayon lines, splashes, runs, abstract shapes, flowers, and fun—and why not? What will happen when you let go to experiment? Discover? Explore? Let's see—you might waste a piece of paper? You might make a mess? A mistake? Look foolish? You might have fun? Passion? Risk something new?

Why are we all so fearful of making mistakes, experimenting, discovering? Were we punished, chided, rejected as young explorers? Or were we conditioned to believe that making a mistake is bad, wrong, awful, stupid—or worse—permanent? Did we feel rejected when we stepped out of line? Or coloured out of the lines? Were we wasteful?

> **It is human nature to experiment, to discover, to test limits, and, in so doing, to grow.**

Pushing boundaries and limits can have startling and delightful results. Sometimes. Making muddy colours on your paper, scrubbing a hole through a painting, testing new techniques, trying different colours, developing chaos in music, finding a new beat, breaking a sculpture and creating a new shape, even turning a work upside down—some might call that daring innovation!

Tension in art is engaging!

And what if the exploration does not yield the hoped-for results? Well, go ahead and try another direction and see what happens.

> *It happens in science, it happens in business,*
> *and it certainly happens in all forms of art:*
> *Innovation results from taking that different path.*

Respond to life with your art

There is much to see. Shadows have their own colours and landscape, rocks sparkle with pink and azure, and clouds are barely white. What colours dwell in the darkness of black?

Breathe what you are seeing into your art. Feel the sounds and the colours and the echoing movement.

Behold the view before you. What do you feel? What is the rhythm like? What lures you? How do objects, colour, and light relate to each other, each being part of a puzzle? Describing what you see depends on the sharpness or softness of your vision and can be the basis of abstraction described only in tone, form, and perhaps colour. Artists are expected to choose between abstraction and realism. Even if we choose, it is not an absolute.

Sometimes I enjoy painting in an abstract way; other times, I take care to represent objects in a recognizable way. It just depends on what I want to do. Feelings, motion, and response direct the strokes of my brush, as well as the choice and placement of colour.

Before starting on a painting, I examine form, light, line, relationships, and composition. I do this by reading, studying other artists' work, looking around, going for walks, meditating, and preparing many preliminary sketches. Sometimes I focus on certain subjects pertaining to upcoming projects. Taking time to observe, to study, and to play with sketches sets me free and helps me to gain confidence for the next project or to take risks in exploring various aspects of my work.

Do I think about all this as I am painting? No, I have done my thinking ahead of time. In painting I am right there in the field, with the trees and birds.

When I am painting expressively, I try to stay with my body sensations and out of my head. My body movements and breathing suggest a pause or completion.

My art experiences parallel my life experiences. As I open new doors in my artistic self, new doors open in my daily life. As I amplify my observation skills through my drawings, I expand my insight. By experiencing new sights, noticing details around me, I see life from an expanded perspective. I take the leap and safely land with a new understanding of myself and my world.

Learning, doing, trying, and experimenting — these are all invigorating, daring, interesting, and fun.

You hate my work! Ouch! I hate my work!

It's one thing to set aside your work to view it, critique it, describe it, and contemplate it or respond to it. It is quite another thing to judge, cross out, tear up, or suddenly toss the work aside.

When I hear that someone has thrown away his work or has furiously scratched it out, crossed it out, or torn it up, it touches me.

> ***Artists are rarely pleased with their pieces as a finished product.***

Taking time to study your work can help you to understand your position when you worked on it. It is a freeze-frame of who you were at that moment, what you felt, how you reacted or didn't react to your environment, and the state of your inner world. Looking at it again, you will see that it probably not only exposes your technical ability at that time, it also may show you how far you have progressed.

Analyzing your work in a supportive environment is paramount. Commonly, we tend to be overly critical of our accomplishments. It is important to expose your work in a supportive environment where helpful comments and suggestions can move you forward. Alone, as each of us knows, we can find reasons to tear our own work apart in seconds.

> ***What every budding or professional artist needs are comments to help build that base of skills and knowledge.***

Art can be a lonely endeavour. We need encouragement from our fellow artists and peers. We need to understand that personal taste is just that. It is not a measure of excellence. In sharing our work with others, especially fellow artists, we are able to see the value and strength of the work.

This takes courage.

Do you have concerns that your new venture into practising art will be criticized? Are you concerned about what others will see in your work? Or whether your work will have value?

I believe that judgments are a matter of opinion. You can set your own parameters, your own standards, and be the judge of your own work. What you produce in your artistic expressions is up to you and ultimately is for you.

Responding expressively

In the expressive arts, the work can be described on the surface without introspective analysis. The maker can describe the types of lines; speed or length of strokes; colour intensity; the spaces; heavy and/or light textures (as on page 49, Practice two). If you are doing this practice with someone, you could ask your partner to respond to the piece in another art form, such as poetry or movement, gestures, sound, or another painting or drawing. It's another way of understanding, witnessing, and acknowledging the work. I have found this method to be a very profound and heartfelt gift for both the giver and receiver. In doing this, we truly are participating fully in the acknowledgment of each other.

DEVELOPING PERSONAL VISION AND UNIQUE STYLE

Follow your intuition! It's right most of the time!

What is your passion?

What grabs your attention?

What excites you?

What angers you?

What is your bliss?

Pursue your dreams. Live those dreams. Express your uniqueness. Entertain yourself with different practices. Explore life's many options and choices. Whatever you want to do artistically—reach for it.

> **Trust yourself, your choices and hunches.**

Consider options and how they feel. You will feel the calm sense of inner knowing and you will feel the rightness of your choice. And synchronicity will entice you along your path.

Take time for this journey.

Spend time alone cultivating your thoughts and developing your path in art. Venture out occasionally to work along with peers; check out exhibitions and museums for stimulation.

The growth of your style and personal vision is an ongoing journey. Don't force it—though you might push it. Be gentle with yourself, follow your heart, listen to yourself, and your style will evolve and develop.

Study the masters and note their techniques. Read and reflect on art history. Be conscious of who and what you respond to. The masters were students their whole lives.

In life as in art, there is always another corner to turn, something else to try out.

Just paint!

Sometimes we need to paint just to paint. Painting is another way of exploring who you are. Paint as if you are going to throw the piece away. Paint as if you will never show this piece. Paint juicy, scratchy, furiously, and with abandon. Keep painting. Practise painting until you feel the flow of the paint. Paint as if you are from Mars and have never seen paint before. Paint with your fingers and toes!

Master the brain critique.

Mind chatter is about wasting time, wasting money, things looking silly and not right, and on and on. We have all heard this inner critic. No one is born with it, although it seems to be part of our innate humanness that our brain defaults to self-denigration. As the inner critic developed, it slowly smothered creative freedom. When you hear the inner critic and its infamous comments, say "thank you" and push onward with your efforts. Let it pass and move on. Eventually the chatter does diminish.

Pretend that you are little again, before you heard the big words of right and wrong. Before you knew what was supposed to be a well-designed masterpiece. And keep painting.

What is in your life and what are you familiar with? What story do you want to tell? Transform your story into your art form.

Art is the voice of your heart. Art is the cry of the soul.

You can communicate through art, sometimes abstractly when photo-realism, familiar structure, and definition would have perhaps choked your intended articulation. How do you see the subject? What speaks to you? How would you describe it in words? Trust yourself. Always follow your intuition first.

It does not matter what art form you choose. Choose what excites you.

If you don't know, experiment. You might find several art forms that feed you and to which you can give your energy. Then choose the medium, tools, and colours that speak to you.

From time to time, you can ask yourself the following questions:

How can I amplify the experience?

When is it time to deconstruct the work? To reconstruct it?

When is it time to take a little break?

When is it time to rely on my foundations and skills?

What is the purpose of the started work?

Whose opinion counts?

Do I have a supportive mentor, one I can trust with my process and vulnerability?

Can I be a mentor? If so, how would I proceed?

Ah, to paint from your heart.

Every idea has validity. No matter what, keep track of your ideas. Journal and sketch so they are there waiting for you when you're ready to try them. Ignore your inner critic and all of your outer critics. Ignore any judgments around those unbelievable ideas. Keep your experiments to yourself if there are any lurking skeptics.

I dare you to venture into the unknown. It feels dangerous to take chances and pioneer new territory, yet what terrible thing could possibly happen? Remember all the others before you who didn't give up trying and pursued what they believed in.

THE UNKNOWN

Often, in the arts, we are not aware of the steps in front of us. We do not know where the path is taking us until we are there. What we do know is the immediate experience.

Enjoy the moment. Enjoy the tactile sensuality of painting, building, carving, spreading, pushing, and pulling.

Don't be content to paint like anyone else, or even try to. You are already unique. After a workshop or class, practise incorporating new skills with your own ideas and systems. Put time into experimenting and you will soon personalize these new skills.

Trust your instincts in your choice of medium, colours, strokes, tools, and methodology. Be aware of your own expression in art and let it prevail.

Even though technique is important, it must follow expression. Your expression is your conviction in the communication of art.

AN INVITATION TO DRAW

There are many ways to study and explore the arts. You can study carefully and deliberately, engage intensely and ferociously, or even dabble casually. You may choose to explore various artistic avenues. Each time you study, you will be increasing your perception and some skill level in each one simultaneously. All your endeavours will benefit from each other.

Materials

Before discussing some exercises, let's consider materials. For drawing, I prefer to use soft lead pencils such as B or 2B, and 4B for good darks. They are not expensive and are available in most art stores. Depending on how you press them, these pencils will respond with a line that can be soft, light, smudged, dark, and/or heavy. Conté is a hard-pressed chalk that can be used for larger drawing. Charcoal is soft and messy and very pliable. Your choice of pencils, conté, or charcoal depends on how you wish to draw and the effect you want to create. Explore and experiment with each of them.

Drawing practices

The connected line exercise was introduced to me when I first started drawing. Practising the connected line exercise develops skills in listening to your body and inner voice with regard to start and finish, pauses, and even the direction and pressure of your pencil on paper. It is the beginning of marking a white page or blank canvas. It is an emptying of chaos in one's life in the form, texture, and expression of the line. The line is the elusive, non-verbal world inside of ourselves. It is a form of expression that has previously been hidden. The connected line is the chance for our body to draw and communicate with us. Sometimes it reveals ideas and solutions. Other times, it suggests memories or horrors. Sometimes it is only a line.

Whatever the connected line exercise does, it seems to get me ready for creativity.

CREATIVE PRACTICE

Drawing with your body, heart, and mind

PRACTICE ONE — CONNECTED LINE EXERCISE

This exercise is a warm-up for drawing. Do it with your eyes closed or half-closed. Instead of your brain controlling the drawing, let your arm, hand, and body take the line, unbroken (pencil not leaving the page), to make shapes.

Just let your body be in the moment and see where it takes the lines.

The process

1. Place a couple of sheets of white bond paper in front of you along with a sharpened pencil. Use sheets measuring at least 8.5 by 11 inches, or a bound sketchbook of the same size.
2. Put on some soothing music and quietly breathe for five to ten minutes. Focus on slowing your breath and your thoughts.
3. When you feel ready, slowly open your eyes and let your body take the pencil.
4. Make lines without lifting pencil from paper.
5. When your body feels done, stop.
6. If you wish, turn the paper over and record your feelings and thoughts about this process.

Take as much time as you wish.

Samples of connected line drawings.

PRACTICE TWO — TRUE CONTOUR DRAWING
(also known as blind contour drawing)

This exercise is a way of intimately touching and studying your object from afar. In this practice, you combine touching and looking. You are expanding your senses and knowledge. You will see and learn about things that will surprise you. Time will not exist. Your world and life as you see it will appear to be changed.

I enjoy this exercise as a warm-up for "modified contour drawing" and getting into the right-brain mode of *spatial thinking*.

Following the contours of your object (without looking at your drawing) is more than outlining. You will find that the lines you draw will follow the shape of your object: round, soft shapes, jagged shapes, points, deep hollows. As you gaze at your object, let your eyes venture into and out of the contour shapes. Stay committed to the idea that your pencil is tracing these movements and it will appear to move in and out, round and about, as well.

This exercise is about getting to know your object of study in an intimate way. It is not about drawing a picture for someone else. Do not worry about what the contour drawing looks like. This exercise is not about creating a finished work of art. It is about heightening your own sensitivities. As we study in this way, I suggest to my students to write the word "true contour" on their drawings to help disarm our worldly critics.

The process

(Read the directions through in their entirety before beginning the exercise.)

1. With sheets of white paper, at least 8 1/2 by 11 inches, or a bound sketchbook of the same size, and a soft lead pencil (B or 2B), sit as close as possible to your object of study. This can be your own hand, a jug, a chair—anything.

2. Focus your gaze on a chosen point on your object of study. Imagine that your pencil is actually touching that point.

3. Put pencil to paper. As you caress the object with your eyes, slowly following contours, crevices, bumps, and lumps, let the pencil travel. Be totally committed to the idea that you are actually touching the object. Keep your gaze fixed only on the object while you move your pencil over the paper, letting the pencil "describe" what you see.

4. Slow down, breathe deeply and slowly, and know that you are doing only this one task right now.

5. As your gaze slowly moves along the object, your pencil will echo those soft, slow movements on the paper. Pencil and eye move together in sync. The pencil will make marks on the paper as your gaze moves slowly over and around the object.

6. Do not look at the paper during this exercise.

7. When you have completely "touched" the whole surface of the object with your pencil, look at your drawing. Note the accuracy of the feelings and textures of the object, even though the lines do not make a photo-realistic representation of the object.

Understand and practise contour drawing before moving on to the next drawing exercise.

A sample of a true contour drawing (top) and a modified contour drawing (bottom) of the same composition.

PRACTICE THREE — MODIFIED CONTOUR DRAWING

This type of drawing applies the same principle as true contour drawing, in that you are combining drawing on paper with lots of focused looking. This exercise continues to develop your perception skills and will give you a more realistic representation of the object you are drawing. In this mode, you pause now and again, keeping the point on your drawing, to check where you are on the page and relate proportions as accurately as possible. Aim to observe the object for 80 percent of the time, and spend the other 20 percent on drawing, so that you will be looking four times longer than you are drawing.

The process

1. With a soft lead pencil (B or 2B) and paper, sit as close as possible to your object of study.
2. Focus your gaze on a chosen point on your object of study.
3. Imagine that your pencil is actually touching the point on your object of study. When you are certain that you have connected your pencil to your object, let the pencil travel and caress the object, slowly following contours, crevices, bumps, and lumps.
4. Pause now and again to compare your drawing to the object. Make slight adjustments to relate proportions as accurately as possible.
5. Be totally committed to the idea that you are actually touching the object.

Slow down, breathe deeply, and know that you are doing only this one thing right now. As your gaze slowly moves along the object, your pencil will echo its shape. Pencil and eye move in sync. Occasionally, look at the lines on your paper, check proportions, and make any minor adjustments. As you practise modified contour drawings, the adjustments become easier, more relaxed, and less frequent.

Note: whenever you stop looking at your object, stop your pencil. This takes some training.

True contour of lilacs in my window.

Modified contour of lilacs in my window.

Finished watercolour of lilacs in my window.

PRACTICE FOUR — CROSS CONTOUR DRAWING

Cross contour drawing is funky! The drawing when finished will look like a topographical map of your object. This exercise takes a lot of time. However, it will revolutionize your drawing and painting skills.

In a cross contour drawing, you map the various contours of your object as well as each subtle change. Later, when you study shading, you will discover that the shadows and highlights of an object follow the cross contour lines, and as you study painting and drawing, you will discover that the painting and drawing implements also follow the cross contour lines.

Cross contour lines interrelate with each other like energy interrelates at all levels. Study Canadian artist Emily Carr's works. She understood the interrelationship of cross contours and energy and the effect these elements had on each other.

The process

1. Begin with a modified contour drawing of your object.
2. Consider how the ellipse shape is formed around the whole object in the sketches on the following page. Following the contours of your object, let the lines follow the shape of your object, round and soft, jagged points, and deep hollows. If it is helpful, lightly sketch the whole ellipse shape in front of and behind the object.
3. As you gaze, venture into and out of the contour shapes of your object.
4. When rendering your contour lines, remain conscious of the line and draw with deliberation and care. Each line is communicating a thought, a sense of direction and shape. Careless lines confuse the message with their multi-directional and inaccurate strokes.

Allow yourself the time to complete this exercise. It is worthwhile and a lot of fun.

*A modified contour drawing of a jade plant
with a few cross contour lines.*

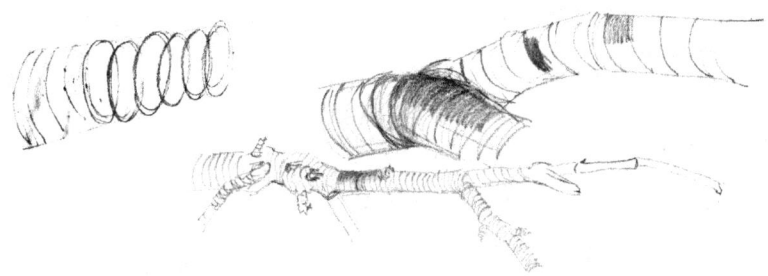

*Try making ellipses on one sample to understand the cross contours.
Then drop the hidden ellipses for the rest of the cross contours.*

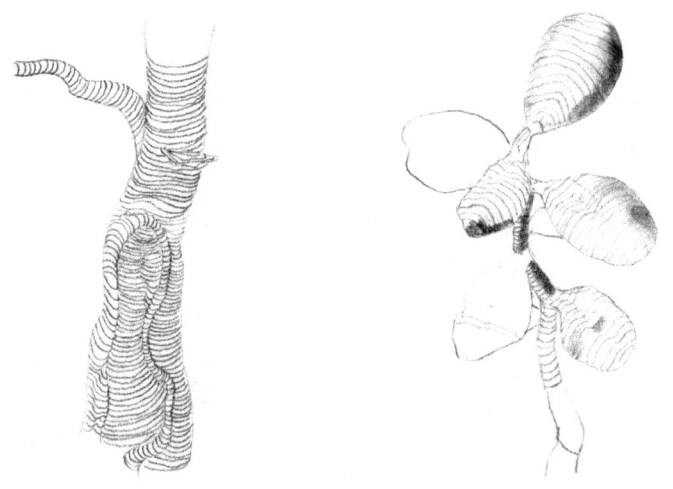

*Cross contour lines can be concave or convex, meaning that the lines
can bend either way, partly because of point of view
and sometimes personal choice.*

PRACTICE FIVE — RESPONSIVE OR GESTURE DRAWING

Responsive drawing is an expressive translation of the object's vitality. This mode of drawing opens up your connection with the object of study and the world around you and will help you to see more accurately and keenly. All your senses and past experiences are involved in the cumulative experience of total seeing. Responsive drawing expands that knowing.

Responsive drawings are intended to be quick drawings. The word "quick" here does not mean hurried. It means that you are drawing responsively, continuously, and impulsively without judgment.

In this mode, you slow down enough to put life's pressures on pause. In this mode, you become attuned to the moving object in front of you. The drawing becomes an energetic relay of the movement and gesture that you witness and feel. You are drawing what the object is doing, not what it looks like.

The process

1. Take a sitting or standing position.
2. Using a soft lead pencil (2B, 3B or softer), or a black medium-tip marker or conté, and a large sheet of paper (preferably a minimum size of 11 by 17 inches—my favourite size is 18 by 24 inches), keep your hand moving, suggesting and mimicking movement.
3. Stand and move your whole body, which accentuates responses (though this is not necessary).
4. Feel the motion you are witnessing in your own body: Feel droops; feel perky; feel jerky; feel power, feel shyness . . . strong strokes, dancing butterfly strokes, jagged, hurtful strokes. What type of stroke is it?

What do you feel? How are you responding?

I have used responsive drawing as a warm-up to painting and to study drawings. I have used it for fun and for building my knowledge. Don't worry about spoilage or image. Use lots of paper. Connect with the whole unit of energy and movement. Have fun.

Pause, relax, take deep breaths and take time to allow yourself the privilege of this journey.

*Example of gesture drawing above
and a detailed study drawing below.*

CREATIVE PRACTICE

Capturing sensation

If the following suggestions are new to you, they may seem awkward. Give them a try regardless.

The process

1. Have coloured pencils, crayons, or markers at hand, together with sheets of paper. (If you have tempera paints available, have them ready, too.)
2. Sit quietly and ponder the list below; your response to any one (or more) may come to you as a sense feeling and an abstract form.
3. Begin with any colour and any shape.
4. Permit your feelings to compel the next shape or colour.

What would a sad line look like?
Try an angry line,
a bold line,
lonely line,
silly line.
Do the colours change, too?

Write or draw your feelings **at present or in memory of an event**.

Write or draw what or how you see **life**.

Write or draw how you taste **a banana**.

Write or draw how you hear **what is around you**.

Write or draw how it feels when you touch **silk**.

Later, try to describe in your journal where these sensory feelings or sensations came from. Are they from thoughts, your heart, reactions, memories, programming, history—or where?

If you like, replace the bolded words with your own and try the exercise again.

To me, spirituality and creativity
are part of a cycle.
When I am creative, I am tapping into
the spiritual part of my existence.
In my spiritual practice, I connect
with creation and receive the energy
that spurs my creativity.

DOING ART TOGETHER

Something wondrous happens when people do art together.

A group can consist of a family, a class, co-workers, or a gathering of friends or strangers. As the art task progresses, participants experience each other in a new way. They are less into thinking and more present with their bodies. Unspoken communication is exchanged at many levels. The art process allows us to transform our worries and leave social judgments behind, permitting us to relate to each other at a more basic and personal level. We see each other differently, and we share parts of ourselves, because somehow this sharing through art feels safer.

> **Working together in art builds trust. Art makes a safe environment that often requires no verbal communication, yet creating art seems to develop a certain caring and harmony and the enjoyment such satisfaction brings.**

In the communal art process, we have discussions and share information; we give encouragement and lend a helping hand; we reach decisions; we share triumphs and fears. Our sensory world is tickled and stimulated. Our perception is expanded within the creative process that accompanies the concentration on each project. Together, we savour the pleasures of this creative process, releasing tensions as we become involved in brush movements and colour and relishing the activity.

By working together, we stimulate each other more than when we work alone. Ideas prompt ideas. Sometimes, it is through the experience of others that we encounter new experiences and rediscover ones that we had left behind. The group creates an energy dynamic exclusive to working together.

It is our nature to make things with our hands. Modern technology has desensitized our hands from the sensuous pleasures of handwriting, crafts, home-style cooking, gardening, and other wonderful tactile activities.

We sit in front of a computer, buy processed, ready-to-heat foods, hire people to do the gardening and weed control, and watch TV instead of involving ourselves in the world around us.

BEING IN THE MOMENT

Drawing and painting are two ways of being totally present in your life. Especially when you draw and paint outdoors. While concentrating on your environment, you become acutely aware of it at that moment. This acute awareness ripples into the rest of your experiences by heightening your awareness of surrounding details—light, smells, sounds, and colours. At sharing time at the end of the day, my students recount in detail their drive home, their morning coffees . . . and how much more they see around them.

Practising art opens your eyes to see more in your life.

When I look back at my sketches, I am transported back to that location and all its details. I recall the temperature, conversations, smells, and other stimulations. It is different from a quick photograph. The time taken in sketching is intense and has slowed down time for that moment. Details become imprinted in the memory bank of the brain.

Time to spread your wings

Sometimes you know what you are looking for.

Sometimes you do not know what you are looking for.

Draw or paint what is comfortable and familiar.

Draw or paint what is uncomfortable and unfamiliar.

In the beginning, having been starved artistically, it is typical to mix our paints with extra fury and flourish, using hot colours, doodling repeatedly, and wanting to include everything—cramming all the fun into one painting over and over again. That is perfectly all right. Enjoy the feasting!

Be irresponsible and responsible at the same time.

Dance, move, sing, drum, run, play your way.

Don't worry if you forget something or do something that wasn't intentional. There are no mistakes as an explorer in art.

Art represents life.

Life is contradictory.

So is art.

Art presents life

Life is contradictory

So is it.

chapter seven

EMBRACING DEATH, EMBRACING LIFE

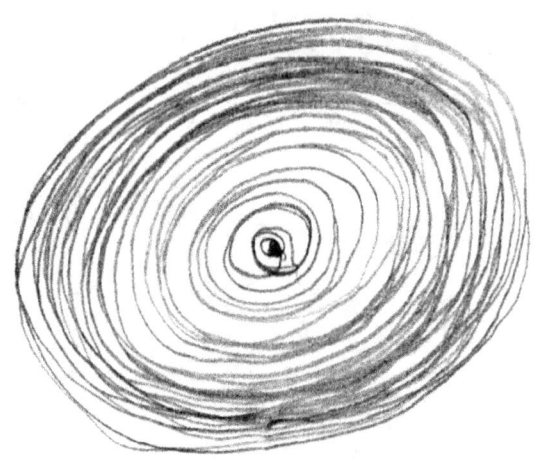

Take a day
to focus on accomplishing nothing,
and you will see that you have
accomplished everything.

EMBRACING DEATH

*With each breath, with each moment,
we move closer to our death.*

First, congratulate yourself for reading this chapter. It takes courage to have a willingness to explore things that are usually avoided. It has taken me a long time to write this chapter. I will present ideas that I hope will inspire you. I will ask you lots of questions.

If you would like to read more about the actual experience of death, being with someone and helping him or her die well, read *Dying Well* by Ira Byock, M.D.[5] He shares personal journeys from his patients and from his vast experience working with hospice and palliative care since 1978.

Embracing the reality of our death on a daily basis with each breath marks the presence and experience of life.

As you read this, keep a few questions in mind: "What would I leave behind, if I died today?" "Does it have value?" and "How can I live more fully with the time I have left?" "Will what I do make others happy?"

To truly live your life is accepting the certainty that we all have when we are born: we will eventually die. Technically that is true, though we rarely contemplate our death or losing someone close to us.

*Why is the fall so precious?
Why do we swoon over flowers? We embrace their
short visit and their fleeting presence with us.*

Why do we want our loved ones to last forever?

Do we hope for our own longevity?

Our Western culture typically does not deal with human death and dying very well. The old are seen as burdens and are not revered for their wisdom, experience, or usefulness. They are put away in separate buildings so we don't have to think about them; or think about aging or dying as often.

We focus on a hopeful future, concentrating on health and well-being. The media seduces us to use cosmetics to look younger longer. Aging is

---

5   Ira Byock, M.D., *Dying Well* (New York: Riverhead Books, 1997).

no longer necessary or fashionable. We know how to eat right, exercise, count calories, and monitor fat intake. The medical profession is ready and able to deal with most of life's challenges. We make jokes about the "D" word in order to diminish its hold on us, using laughter to insulate us from the fear. My friends from Israel share their popular comeback line: "I'm going to kill you!" They say it all the time to each other, out of exclamation, fun, razing, and/or affirmation. They tell me I would be horrified if I knew how often they said it to each other. For them, it's a way to desensitize themselves to all the killing and death they experience on a daily basis.

We can be so immersed in our busyness, achievements, and work that we easily bury the topic of death. We can watch movies, play video games, and buy pre-made dinners. We are a Bluetooth society, linked with electronics. We have become more insular and separate from each other as a community. Our communication is less face to face and more through a keyboard and screen.

We equate living with doing and gathering, not being. Acquiring things—status, a house, a position—are priorities. Sitting still in nature or exploring trails and rivers is uncommon. Purpose and value are hidden somewhere. Random acts of kindness are noted when I wonder why they are not commonplace.

FEAR OF DEATH

Fear of the unknown

People dying of a terminal disease have two primary fears: experiencing pain while dying; and dying alone. In our society, we can medically provide pain-free dying and hospice care. Once these fears are eliminated, it is amazing how rich opportunities surface to deepen relationships. The experience for the individual and his or her relationships can deepen to a point of bliss and peace.

In my family household, it seemed my father cried for only fifteen minutes at the news of his father's death in Germany. It was scary when the pillar of the family broke down and cried. It was weird. The topic was taboo. Curious questions were hushed. We all moved on, and the sooner we got into our daily routines, the better. Funeral homes were a fascination and seemed macabre. The news of the deaths of my grandparents and various aunts and uncles was announced. Sometimes a trip was planned to attend the funeral.

I was so afraid of death as a child and young adult that thoughts of the possibility left me clammy, nauseous, and shaky. No one talked about it; no one answered my questions. I could only file them away in my brain somewhere. The trouble with that was, the topic of my upcoming death lurked in my brain in an unorganized way, causing a lot of trouble for me. The underlying thoughts and emotions affected my actions.

I wanted to talk about death. Even at Sunday school, no one wanted to talk about dying, only about being saved. It was not enough of an answer for me. Since that time, I have learned that spirituality is a personal and individual quest. Our interpretation and experience of life and death is uniquely our own.

Hopefully, asking yourself the following questions will inspire conversations with you, your family, and your loved ones. In all this awareness, it will also help you live more in the moment and treat your own life and every morning as precious and an opportunity. It will help you live well and feel good about your life.

The questions can help to inspire you and to ease your loved ones around you, whether in your living, dying, or death; and in their own living and dying journey.

- Why is it that some terminally ill people say they are truly living since they found out the news of their illness?
- When someone has had a miraculous recovery or a close call, why do they embrace their lives in a fuller, more meaningful way?
- Does life need to be taken away to be appreciated?
- Do we all need to wait for such a chance, or can we learn from those around us?
- Can we realize that we have only a short time on this earth?
- Can we have the courage to look death in the eyes so that we can live to the fullest and make this time meaningful?

Our own death and dying is not a particular topic that we enjoy discussing. From a distance, as Western society, we are fascinated and captivated by the whole topic. Look at the books that are read, the movies produced, the media coverage on capital punishment, abortion, and the right to die. What could these opinions about values and morality around death indicate? Is it a way to acknowledge the topic without actually personalizing it? Is it a way of denying reality by discussing it at arm's length when someone else has died?

One of the hardest parts about death is the loss and grief we feel about it. Death and loss are not the same.

In the grieving part, we are missing the lives that have gone, the lost dreams, new economic realities, loneliness, and other ramifications of the loss. We may or may not analyze our own mortality.

This chapter is really about *living*. Living deliberately is a sound idea; but implementing it is quite another thing.

How deliberate is our living? How purposeful? How giving? Who teaches us to die? Who teaches us to live? Who teaches us to die *well*? Who teaches us to live *well*?

Every day, we are engaged in the "process" of how the end of our lives will be, whether or not we are conscious of it.

Ask yourself, "How do I live in the present?"

As I have been sharing throughout this book, living is experiencing all feelings. The unpleasant ones are not much fun, but they are just as important and valuable to our human survival and growth as the pleasant ones.

Stephen Jenkinson asks some great questions in his DVD and book, *Griefwalker*. Refer to the resources at the back of this book. I have modified the questions in this chapter slightly for our purposes and I invite you to modify them to suit you.

Soul Destiny

If not this trail,
which trail?

If not these woods,
which forest?

Crystal lace frames
a frozen palace
secrets rushing under
icy blankets,
to the end or
to the source?

If not these waterfalls,
which waterfalls?

Uncertain dizzy path
pauses in delightful tastes.
Searches falter at crossroads
yearning for a sure fever.
Fog hangs suspended
till sunlight commands evaporation.

Does it all have to matter?

If not this answer,
which answer?
If not me,
then who?

CREATIVE PRACTICE

Put these ideas into a journal.

What are you afraid of?

Death?

The dying process?

If you could, how would you like to die?

What are the things you would like to say? To whom?

Do you have amends to make?

Any reconciliations?

Pick one question: Could you write a poem about it? What would the question look like in streamers of colour?

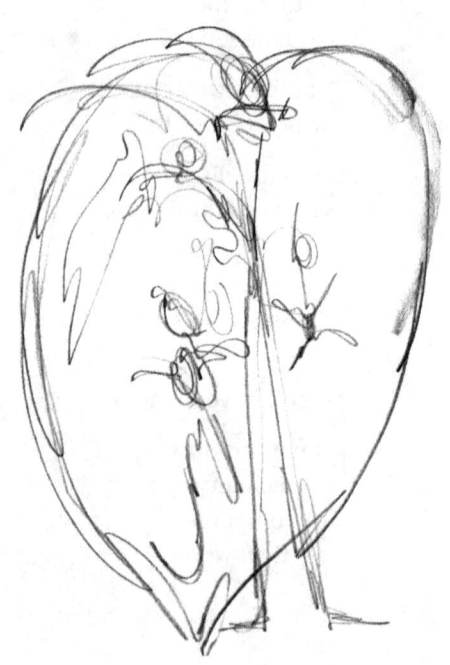

CREATIVE PRACTICE
Put these ideas into a journal.

Imagine yourself with all the body sensations and only one or two months to live.

How would you spend it?

How does it feel?

Who is around you?

What do you see?

What are your convictions about love? About the soul?

What does your destiny mean to you?

What are your opinions on living and dying, and where did they come from? Family? Culture? Society?

CREATIVE PRACTICE

Story of your Life

This is an amazing exercise, introduced to me by Ruth Howard of Jumblies Theatre. I use it regularly in the workshops I faclitate.

Arrange to be in silence. For this exercise, you'll need a large piece of paper, at least 18 by 24 inches. Oil pastels work well with this exercise and they are quite economical. Have various colours handy.

You will be asked to think of certain things in your life and to document them. You can draw a symbol or a small picture or use a word to represent the answer. Consider more the shape of the line and the colour that a symbol might best represent what you would like to document. Take your time. There is no right or wrong way to do this exercise. I have seen it done and have facilitated these practices for many years, and each life story is unique.

In this life story, you will discover your mentors, inspirations, and strengths.

Slowing your breath down a little bit, first cover the paper with a light coating of pale pastel, patterns if you like, as you will be adding images on top of this first layer.

- Mark a place on the paper representing your birth, where and when you are born, using either an object or words, then put your name or nickname beside it.
- Add the gifts you were born with, either words or images.
- Add the curses you were born with, either words or images (curses could be flaws, whether in yourself, your family, or your surroundings).
- Take some deep breaths.
- Make a road or a path to indicate your journey.
- On this path, put three to five significant events that come to mind.
- For each event, how old were you?
- What were the obstacles, if any?
- What got you through? What was the experience like?

- What were the safe havens? What protected you?
- List any guides or mentors who helped along the way (can be different for each event); were there any special people?
- What were the magic words? Lullabies? Phrases, quotes? Any word that was soothing? Maybe a song, poem?
- What would be some power words for these events? Character words like determination, grace, compassion, creativity, dependability, discernment, faith, endurance, flexibility, forgiveness, generosity, gentleness, gratitude, honour, humility, justice, loyalty, patience, responsibility, sensitivity, tolerance, honesty, wisdom?
- And your future: Do you have some sense of the next adventure?
- Do you have a question/riddle for the future? Curiosity about anything? Wondering?
- Are there any connections to the pieces?
- Before you stop, pause, breathe deeply, slowly a few times and consider if there is anything else you would like to add.

Further reflections:
- What parts felt comfortable?
- What parts felt uncomfortable?
- What are you curious about?
- What surprised you?

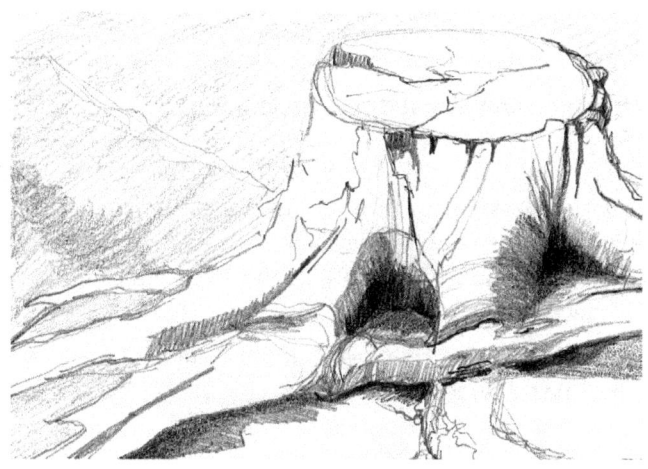

KNOWING THAT YOU ARE GOING TO DIE

Would it make a difference to you to be given notice of a terminal disease, a potentially terminal disease, a degenerative disease, or ailing health? We may or may not wish to analyze our own mortality, but it can be a fruitful exercise.

People who have been there are the resources for the following.

If you know that you are dying slowly, you can take this time as an opportunity to think about some of the questions below. Your focus is on the body and on the disease process.

- What influences your views?
- What influences your ideas about dying?
- How do fears about pain and symptoms change your thinking?
- What about the idea of going to sleep and not waking up?
- What about the presence of loved ones when you die, or do you want your privacy?
- What will happen to those left behind?
- Will you plead with God?
- What does the passage of time mean to you?
- What does knowing that you are dying mean to you?
- Do you want to know?
- What good can come from this?
- If you thought about dying, could this help you with living?

The reality of death can stop me in a moment. All of a sudden, things are not as important anymore. However, my time and my relationships are very precious. We are here for a fleeting moment in time and space, so I ask myself, what do I want to do with that? Pass time? Collect things? Work at something I hate, or even dislike?

For me, the richness, the "rightness," and the value of my purpose and mission give me fulfillment and meaning.

A life lived following my passions has meaning. Working in hospice with grief and bereavement has given me the gift of being more present. I treasure each moment.

Death is an ongoing life experience.

You are pregnant and then you are not.

Ending creates a beginning.

You have a baby, a toddler, a preschooler, and then you do not.

Life creates movement.

How do you assimilate and process natural, everyday experiences that have a beginning and then morph into something unexpected, unwarranted, and/or unwanted?

Movement creates change.

Change creates chaos.

Each day is an adventure in the unknown—every single moment. None of us really knows when we will meet our death. Each day, each moment is all we have, and to live our best is all we can do.

Chaos finds natural harmony.

The natural order of things cannot help but find balance.

Harmony expands to peace, death, and pure love.

Being practical

If you are an adult with any kind of assets or dependents, it is important to have a will in Western society. Why? Because it is your life and you are responsible for it and everything in it all the time, not just when you are elderly. I hated preparing my will. The process made me face the unpleasant reality of this temporary state of living. Well, the will is done, and my children and family will have it easier because of it. When wills are not done or updated, there can be great conflict and grief within a family.

Have you assigned a power of attorney, giving clear guidelines of your wishes, should you become incapacitated? Why? Because it requires you to give serious thought to how you want to live your life when you have no control over it. It also gives you the opportunity to find someone who will respect your wishes should the unthinkable happen.

Are you an organ donor? If so, under what conditions? Will you be a living donor if you are on life support and terminal? Have you registered and have you made your wishes known to family and friends?

Do you want cremation? If so, have you made the necessary arrangements? Or do you prefer burial? Have you selected your "final resting place"?

The above is all about living in the moment. When all these issues are taken care of, you will find that living will be about taking care of the details, enjoying every experience, and letting it go when it is completed so you can go to the next and the next and the next . . . up to and including your death.

Almost Whole

One day I came to you almost whole—
A gem was hidden in my soul.

Butterfly kisses began to melt
an ancient wounded crusty core.

Over and over and over again,
Smoothing, soothing memories' lore

Seductive ecstasy, pushing chatter
into a need that seemed to matter.

One day I came to you almost whole—
a gem was hidden in my soul.

Raging yes-no madness
surfaced old wounds raw,

Invested torment gained in
primal cells shaking from the law

vulgar tearing at shame,
relentless hunger, ignoring pain.

One day I came to you almost whole—
a gem was hidden in my soul.

Ripping away, searching for truth,
leaving home at great cost,

I cried to the heavens to soothe
a happiness so totally lost.

Time answered with new sight,
love seemed to bring its own light.

One day I came to you almost whole—
a gem was hidden in my soul.

Sparkles blitzed the rubble,
a brilliant facet caught my eye.

Love, one could not have dreamed of,
in a single sigh.

Soft nothings whispered through my hair,
wind sweetly tingled my skin bare.

A gem no longer hidden in my soul—
this day I come to you mostly whole.

EMBRACING GRIEF AND LOSS

The only way out of grief is through it.

Typically, in my experience, our Western society does not handle grief very well. Our media hypes us into believing we must feel better and live bigger with things. We are coached in the need to control any negativity and unpleasant feelings. Positive thinking is promoted to a point that it can negate the full spectrum of human emotions. Feeling better quicker is seen as strength. Having real feelings tends to be awkward and people around us don't know how to act.

I was brought up to be stoic; unhappy feelings like grief and depression were a weakness. As a young adult, I felt confused, unstable, and incapable of handling life. This greatly affected how I lived my life and the choices I made. My feelings were so tangled they roiled regularly in my stomach, creating anxiety and insomnia.

Usually, loss is a shock, and any work on grief or therapy would start after a minimum of three months. Before that time, let yourself or others just be in the grieving process. Be gentle.

I hope this chapter will give you some insight on how to handle grief, whether it's your own or someone else's. There are research groups that support grief processing. Most times, groups are magnificently helpful in the healing process. Talk to the facilitator and establish if the group is a fit for you.

Grief is a process; it takes its own time. You don't ever get over it; however, you learn to manage it so you can have a happy, fulfilled life.

Grief is a natural expression of love for the person who is lost.

Lives are forever changed by the loss of someone we love.

Normalizing grief and loss

Experiencing grief, deep sorrow, and pain, comes from experiencing loss.

What kind of loss? Any loss: separation, moving, death; loss of health, of a body part, of mental and/or physical capacity; loss of a career and/or status, a close pet, a job, a team, a dream. A loss of competition, even an expectation; new economic realities; loneliness and other costs might have accompanied the loss. Our loss cannot be compared to another's. It has no measurement, no scale. We are individual in how we each experience loss.

Grief and sadness are part of the unpleasant feelings that as a society we mostly have convinced ourselves not to feel or dwell in. This results in buried and unorganized, unhappy feelings that have nowhere to go except to pop up in strange ways later on that we don't recognize as the original feelings.

Grief can manifest itself in so many ways. In the group work I do, participants have shared that they have experienced nightmares, insomnia, exhaustion, nervousness, anger, tears, no feelings, overwhelmed feelings, mixed-up feelings, hunger, loss of appetite, unfocused states, mixed-up thinking, headaches, forgetfulness, and many more. There can be a tendency to get sick. Perhaps we have shut down so much of our feeling that we feel flat, shallow, and dull. These feelings come and go with varying intensity and frequency.

In my grief and loss workshops, the more we allow our feelings expression, unedited and unabridged, the easier the unpleasant feelings can flow through us and move away to make room for other, more pleasant feelings.

We are feeling humans again and feel alive.

As I have been sharing throughout this book, living is experiencing *all* feelings. The harder ones are not as much fun; however, they are just as important and valuable to our human survival and growth.

The following is a brief outline from a handout I give to participants in the grief and loss recovery programs that I facilitate.

- **Listen.**
- **Let grief have its own path.**
- **Be yourself. Be honest.**
- **Take good care of yourself.**

Listen to the grief over and over again: to all of grief's story(ies); the concerns; the worries; the guilt; the confusion; the anger; the sadness; and the fears. Have patience. Don't try to fix anything. Just listen—don't lecture or advise.

The best we can do, for ourselves and another, is to fully acknowledge the feelings and the pain. According to Carl Rogers, a well-known twentieth-century psychologist, when a person feels accepted and understood, this is the beginning of true healing. Rogers's research revealed that it is a rare experience to feel accepted and understood when you are feeling fear, rage, grief, anxiety, or jealousy. And it is this very acceptance and understanding that heals. By genuinely hearing the depth of emotional pain and respecting the individual's ability to find her own answer, we are giving her the greatest gift. This provides the individual the opportunity for empowerment, to build her resilience and to discover her unique potential.

Believe in the other's ability to heal. Don't push.

Respect the need to talk or to be silent.

We all have the right to talk about our grief. Talking about our grief will help us to heal. Seek out others who will allow you to talk about your grief as much as you want and as often as you want.

If you can't be a listener for someone, gently let him know that you cannot do this at the moment, but encourage him and support him in finding someone who can.

No one gets over grief; however, we learn how to live with it.

Let grief have its own path. Everyone processes and experiences grief differently. Grief has different intensities, different symptoms, and different times. No one can predict any of these things for anyone.

If you push grief away, ignore it, rush it, negate it, deny it, file it, and/or pretend anything at all about your grief, it will only cause the grief to fester inside. If grief doesn't have a chance to move, it will pop out in other unpredictable and unfavourable ways, until it is acknowledged and processed.

Be with grief. If someone is trying to suspend her grief, encourage her to feel it. Grieving people don't always initiate; let them know ways that you can help.

People have shared with me that the most scary part about feeling grief is that they are worried they won't ever feel better or that they won't be able to stop crying.

By allowing grief its own path—as unpleasant, awkward, uncomfortable, and sad as it is—the wave will pass on its own. My experience is that the intensity of the grief changes. The unpleasant feeling lasts for a shorter time and generally becomes less intense over time. (Although it is mostly unpredictable.)

Sometimes we worry that someone close to us is doing "strange" things to cope with their grief—for example, sitting in a closet, sleeping with photos, picking up obsessive-compulsive habits. As long as these actions are not hurting anyone, then let them be. My experience as a grief counsellor is that most of the time these habits dissipate as the feelings of grief get acknowledged and begin to progress. If the behaviour is hurting someone, then it is best to seek professional guidance.

> *We live with change and loss all our lives.*
>
> *What we can do is learn how to manage our grief, our changes, and our losses. We can learn how to live with what we have.*
>
> *There can be strength and joy in that, one moment at a time.*

Be yourself. Be honest. Let others know you are upset, too. Be curious. Be natural. Listen with your heart, with undivided attention, with your eyes and ears. Do not give answers if you do not have them.

You have the right to experience your own unique grief. No one else will grieve in exactly the same way you do. When you turn to others for help, don't allow them to tell you what you should or should not be feeling.

You have the right to feel a multitude of emotions: confusion, disorientation, fear, guilt, anger, and relief are just a few of the emotions you might feel as part of your grief journey. Others may try to tell you that feeling angry, for example, is wrong.

Surround yourself with people who will accept your feelings without conditions.

You have the right to experience "grief attacks." Sometimes, out of nowhere, a powerful surge of grief may overcome you. This can be frightening and unbalancing; however, it is natural.

I knew someone who broke down eight years after losing someone. This individual cried for three solid days and then stopped. Every person is different.

Take good care of yourself. Consider your own process and your own limitations.

You have the right to be tolerant of your physical and emotional limits. Feelings of loss and sadness are exhausting. Respect what your body and mind are telling you. Pace yourself. When you are processing deep emotions, self-care is even more important than usual. Make sure you get enough rest. Plan to eat well. Trust your body. Don't allow others to push you into doing things you don't feel ready to do.

Reach out to others as you do the work of mourning.

Don't be afraid to have fun. Laughter is good medicine.

Coping with grief

Everyone copes with grief differently. Self-soothing activities vary from bubble baths, to calling a friend, reading, watching a movie, shopping, eating comfort foods, drinking, being with pets, and so on.

There are many ways to cope and to temporarily distract ourselves. Sometimes we need to take deliberate breaks to take a pause from the pain and suffering. Almost any distraction could be harmless when done in moderation. If the distraction hampers your coping with life and relationships, then the distraction may be harmful and needs to be looked at with consideration.

You have the right to make use of ritual. Artmaking can be a ritual; as can a bonfire ceremony. The funeral ritual does more than acknowledge the death of someone loved. It helps provide you with the support of caring people. More important, the funeral is a way for you to mourn. Some people like to plan a celebration of life or a memorial. If others tell you that rituals such as these are silly or unnecessary, don't listen.

You have the right to embrace your spirituality. If faith is a part of your life, express it in ways appropriate to you. Allow yourself to be around people who understand and support your beliefs. Find someone to talk with who won't be critical of your feelings of hurt and abandonment.

You have the right to search for meaning. You may find yourself asking, "Why did he or she leave? Why this way? Why now?" Some of your questions may have answers, but some may not. And watch out for the clichéd responses some people may give you. Well-intended comments like, "I know how you feel," or "Think of what you have to be thankful for," are not helpful. You do not need to accept them, as they may negate what you are feeling. This sounds pretty tough, though most people in our Western society are not well versed in difficult, sensitive situations.

You have the right to treasure your memories. Memories are among the best legacies that exist after the death of someone loved. You will always remember. Instead of ignoring your memories, find others with whom you can share them.

You have the right to move toward your grief and heal. Reconciling your grief will not happen quickly. Remember, grief is a process, not an event. Be patient and tolerant with yourself and avoid people who are impatient and intolerant with you. Neither you nor those around you must forget that the loss of someone loved changes your life forever.

CREATIVE PRACTICE

- Gather some old magazines, a glue stick, felt markers, scissors, and a large piece of 18 by 24-inch Bristol board or stiff paper.
- Make a collage of your experiences of your loss: the good experiences, funny memories, and any unpleasant experiences, even painful memories.
- What were some favourite activities you did together?
- What were the favourite meals? Colours? Clothes?
- Do any special places, holidays, or events come to mind?
- Character traits? Funny habits? Hobbies?
- What things make you angry?
- When you are done and when it feels right, share your collage with a close friend.
- Try journalling what you learned.

HOW DO CHILDREN GRIEVE?

Children grieve in ways similar to, and different from, adults. Like adults, children experience grief physically, emotionally, cognitively, spiritually, and behaviourally. As with adults, they experience grief as a roller coaster. However, since they are still developing, they may revisit their grief as their understanding of loss deepens.

Children live more in the moment than does the average adult. They believe that their discomfort and pain will be long-lasting. They do not have the life experience that adults do, so their expressions of grief may be intense and episodic. As they cannot articulate very well—if at all—their feelings, they feel terrible, mixed up, and uncomfortable sharing. They usually think something is wrong with them. Among the manifestations of grief might be regressive behaviours, acting out, sleep disturbances, or, at school, changes in grades or attitudes.

Expressive Art Therapy is an effective medium that addresses many grief issues through art, music, movement, dance, and drama. Expressive Art Therapy offers a safe way for kids to communicate when they can't find their voice or a way to express their loss and pain. The arts is a vehicle to express the feelings and get them outside of oneself. Once that is done, the maker can look at the art process more objectively.

Any child old enough to love is old enough to grieve.

What about teens?

For many teens who are experiencing grief, it comes at a time when they feel invincible, powerful, and ready to take on the world. A significant loss can shatter this myth and throw them into a state of panic and doubt, causing them to question their beliefs, plans, and hopes for the future. As this stage is naturally high with emotion, a reaction to loss is even more intense. Teens will vary in how they react: They may be moody, aggressive, clingy, engage in wild risk-taking, or unwilling to take any risks at all, along with other symptoms of grief already mentioned. Teens often will feel guilty for their behaviours, or angry that they survived.

As a parent, you might want to "fix" or take their pain away. It's important to allow youth to work through their pain. Be there to support them when they need you.

Basic principles in helping children grieve

- Remember, an important influence on children and youth are the actions and responses of the adults around them.
- Stay in touch.
- Listen. Allow kids to teach you about their experiences of grief; they are all unique and have their personal journey.
- Teach them how to tell you how they feel.
- Don't assume that children of the same age will act the same.
- Don't lie or tell half-truths. Be honest and give them as much as they may be able to understand for their age.
- Be authentic with your own grief and feelings. In this you are teaching them that even as adults we have pain—that pain and suffering are a natural part of the human condition.
- Don't wait for a big tell-all. When is it ever the "right" moment?
- Encourage kids to ask questions.
- Understand that when kids don't always act sad it is because they can't absorb all the pain at once.
- Allow children to participate in rituals.

Although we try to protect children from death and loss, children experience a range of losses even in childhood. These losses can include separations and divorce, deaths of persons or pets, or other losses such as health or moving to a new school.

As children experience these losses, they will grieve. This grief must be supported, not ignored. By supporting them, we help children not only adapt to the immediate loss, but also to learn adaptive skills that will help them face inevitable and subsequent losses.

How do children understand death?

Death is a very difficult concept for young children to understand. They struggle with ideas like inevitability, universality, non-functionality, and the irreversibility of death. They still might grapple with understanding what they believe happens after death. They are developing not only cognitively and spiritually, but also emotionally and socially. At young ages, children tend to view death through their own perspective: "What does this death mean for me?"

Later, they become more empathetic. Similarly, they are better able to understand and sustain feelings. Young children have a "short feeling span"; they can sustain strong feelings for only a short time.

How should I discuss loss and death with a child?

First, always be honest and straightforward. The stories we weave to comfort children often confuse them. Let the child's questions guide the discussion. What do they want to know? What can they understand? What do they need to know? As always, death is best first discussed outside of a crisis. Take opportunities from TV or stories to begin discussions about loss and life cycles. Ask your local librarian and hospice centres for resources appropriate to children at different ages. Some of these books or videos will help in educating a child about loss; others are helpful for a child experiencing grief.

Should a child visit someone in a hospital? Should he/she go to a funeral?

Children, as soon as they can sit through a visit, should have a choice. For that choice to be meaningful, children need information and options. Explain what they are likely to see. Give them choices. They can visit, call, or make a tape or card. They can go to the funeral visitation, service, or cemetery. Make sure there is someone around who can support the child. And provide opportunities later to discuss his/her experiences.

What does a grieving child need?

The child needs a great deal of support and understanding. When the loss is someone very close, like a parent or sibling, others in the family may be too involved in their own grief to support the child. Counselling, groups, grief camps, and simply solid support from friends and family might be helpful. A local hospice may be a good source of information about available recourses.

Warning signs of complications

Sometimes youths and children (or adults) struggle more than usual with grief. All the following signs contain elements of healthy grieving, although problems can arise with intensity and elapsed time since the loss; and to a degree where healing is not present, and the situation is a threat to well-being.

Consider in these cases the help of a professional:
- Minimal or a total lack of emotional expression regarding the loss
- Prolonged inability to recognize that the loss has happened; living as if the loss has not occurred at all; attachment to an object replacing the loss
- Extreme reactions of anger and guilt that continue over time to a point of no healing or mourning
- A significant change in health
- Extended depression, tension, agitation, insomnia, and feelings of worthlessness

Cracked Linoleum

cool wet wood,
plum and apple compote
bubbling lazily on the cast iron stove.
Lace curtains frame iron windows.
In the distance his tractor
putters home along the cobblestone road,
bringing the cows home.
They become my pets.

Maybe by holding my breath,
I can hold time,
hold him,
hold myself,
hold the calm.

The cows mosey along,
the pigs squeal greetings to his village soup.
His voice, soft, raspy,
a little broken and contemplative
sips warm milk.
We touch, comparing our hands,
and laugh,
his thumb is twice the size of mine.
Our rhythm is so easy—
His eyes twinkle.
Red currants burst so sweet
with slight sour humour,
take me back to his garden.

I want to save it.
restore it,
hold it.
Maybe if I don't breathe
I can hold the time,
hold him,
hold myself,
hold the calm.

I feel lost, yet I don't feel lost,
maybe he is who I am.

All the words we didn't speak
are spoken now.

CREATIVE PRACTICE

Journalling Feelings

These creative practices are designed for a young person; however, you could do them, too. The purpose is to bring about some self-discovery of self-awareness and to express feelings.

- In your journal, check in how you feel each day.
- Write or draw a picture about at least three feelings a day (good and not-so-good feelings, and try to include the different feelings you have) and in point form describe the situation that caused that feeling, or draw a picture.

This is an awareness exercise; there is no right or wrong in this exercise.

Who I Am

Write or draw a picture about THREE things that:

- I like or love
- People who are important to me
- I worry about
- I hope for
- Words that describe me
- That make me angry
- That frustrate me
- That make me feel lonely
- That make me sad
- That I feel good about
- I would I like to do
- I am good at
- That help me feel safe or protected
- That are important to me

CREATIVE PRACTICE

What's Left?

Take your time and answer the questions in your own order. This exercise is best done after some time has passed and some work has been done processing grief.

Take a notebook and dedicate it to writing everything you have, everything you did receive, and everything you have left.

Go on a treasure hunt of your life.

- How were your needs met? How are they being met now?
- What resources do you have?
- What are your strengths?
- What did you learn from your losses and from what you endured?
- How did your losses shape you?
- What are your talents? What are you good at?
- Can you still hear? Can you still see?
- Do you have your sense of smell and taste?
- Can you walk? Can you run?
- If you cannot walk, do you have a wheelchair so you can get around?
- What do other people see that you have?
- What do they admire in you?
- What do you like about yourself?
- What have you been complimented on (even if you don't believe it)?
- What have you accomplished?

Your goal is to make this list longer than your list of losses.

In your notebook, keep adding all the things you have and are grateful for.

chapter eight

MAPPING YOUR JOURNEY

When will you get the respect

that you deserve?

It will begin when you give it to yourself.

BECOMING WHO YOU ARE

So, you've read the book. Now what?

I have noticed that people get inspired, make some changes for a while; although as life events unfold, old habits prevail. Perhaps the habits are protection and security. Perhaps it's too hard, or the new habits are not strong enough, need more support, or the changes aren't believable.

This chapter summarizes the book and offers some ways of continuing support.

Be open

Be open to how your desires unfold. Your wishes might not look exactly like you envisioned. Be open to different points of view. Be open to receiving knowledge and help from unlikely places. Use the exercises that best suit you.

- Concentrate on your breathing. Be grateful for every breath.
- Slow down.
- Take your own time.
- Listen to yourself first, then to everything else.
- Practise.
- Remain curious.
- Practise.
- Move your body.
- Take care of yourself; get to know what that entails for you.
- Get to know the truth about yourself.
- Practise.
- Embrace love. Illuminate your life with love. Love holds the brightest light on truth. Love people around you, talk about love, think about love, read about love, encourage love, seek out love in being kind and loving. Let your love emerge in acts of kindness and tenderness for whomever and whatever is around you.
- Practise.

Notice what it is that you do that is most helpful for you.

CONTINUE TO BALANCE AND LOVE LIFE

Life happens on its own. We have chances and can make some opportunities. We are left with choices. We are left with attitude.

How do we keep balanced?

In order to continue to maintain balance, we need to keep an awareness about who we are and what is around us; we need to stay present. It is important to be disciplined and committed to self-care. My experience has shown that this is extremely important.

Sometimes that awareness goes astray when we are consumed by a serious situation, extreme stress, and emotional turmoil. How do we regain our balance if we have lost our equilibrium?

It is extremely important to build support strategies for ourselves to fall back on, or to cling to when we are flailing about. We do much better when we build our resilience on a daily basis, get encouragement, and enjoy regular successes.

- Build several support systems for yourself, especially when you are feeling strong, so they are there when you feel otherwise.
- Know that you are special and deserve a great life.
- Know that life is a great gift.
- Know that you can learn new habits and new ways of thinking.
- Slow down so you can hear your heart. Then start following it again.
- Continue to begin every day with curiosity.
- Practise for the rest of your life.

All this rekindles passion in your life.

What Feeds a Mountain?

What feeds a mountain?

Ancient patience wearing smooth,
a coat of amour no longer shiny.
Crevice wounds shift and shake
As bare bones rattle her story.

What feeds a mountain?

Wind-thrown alpine gardens awaken a path,
trees too stubborn to give up their grip,
grasses, bushes, moss,
all feel they have the right.

What feeds a mountain?

Hooves trample, stampede, and play,
mindless crashing of rocks.
Holes are burrowed in fury,
Scat has no impulse or thought.

What feeds a mountain?

Storms thunder rage, then leave.
Silence chills, haunted with secrets.
Clouded perspective at dizzying heights,
The wind gasps.

What feeds a mountain?

Relentless sun melts the questions,
tears rush below the surface,
murky waters steal
the soul no one knows.

What feeds a mountain?

Glacier ice stings the surface,
a heart burns at the core.
Weighted under dark rubble
an exhausted sigh whispers longingly.

What feeds a mountain?

STRENGTHENING INNER AND OUTER HAPPINESS

Inner happiness

I view the world from the inside looking out.

Building the inner core

Throughout the book, I have offered various ways to build and understand oneself.

My memories and point of view are the lenses from which I view the world around me. How I feel about myself determines how I react and act and how I make choices; it determines my attitude. What I believe forms my opinions and how I interpret what I read and hear.

As I change my point of view and open up my heart, I see people and life around me in a new way.

What do some daily practices look like? I would suggest that you choose the exercises that were most helpful for you and implement them on a daily basis.

DAILY PRACTICE

Small Steps

Health is a state of complete physical, mental, and social well-being, not just the absence of disease. I do not take my mental health and overall well-being for granted. I support myself with a disciplined daily practice and take care of myself in a holistic way. I have learned through experience that if I live in a holistic way, I thrive and feel great! I need to take care of the emotional, mental, physical, and spiritual aspects of myself. I can miss a day, but if I let my self-care regime slip, I can sink into some unpleasant states.

Also be aware that levels of well-being fluctuate in quality and intensity.

I am healthy; I have a simple, beautiful home in a beautiful area of the world. I felt lucky. Logically, according to my blessings and gratitude list, I should be dancing and springing for joy every day — or most days, at the very least. Yet I didn't feel this ecstatic joy. So how could I achieve this?

I have had many traumatic experiences at the beginning of my life. Trauma, loss, stress, grief, drama, worry, anxiety, and depression took up a lot of space in my memory banks. I refer to this space as "trauma property." My default experience of life went to this dominant memory bank. Even though I was beginning to understand a lot of this trauma, my triggers led me there most times on those well-worn neural pathways.

When the trauma property dominates space in your brain, it blocks playfulness and joy. As we have read, any block is an inhibitor. It can totally or partially block the good feelings, in various ways, in various times and situations, and to varying degrees. This is a place of awareness where you could use some support. When one has blocks, it's difficult to see all aspects clearly on one's own.

The body experiences excitement and anxiety in a very similar way. So if the brain has a larger trauma property, anxiety and the body's reactions to it will be the default feeling for excitement.

The body also experiences tenderness / deep love and sadness in a very similar way. So if the brain has a larger trauma property, when you feel deep love, it may appear as if you are sad.

If one is unaware of these similarities, the body sensations can be very confusing. For example, when good things are happening, the body reacts as if the situation were bringing about anxiety responses.

If your brain default is trauma, then all those feelings—good and bad—will go to the trauma property first and you will react to good things in your life the same way as you would to unpleasant things: with insomnia, over- or under-eating, tension, depression, over- or under-working, and so on.

The goal is to give the joy space a place—a property—and then to make the joyful property bigger and stronger.

How was I going to make the joy property bigger than the trauma property in my brain?

One wise counsellor had me recount positive stories and experiences to him. He suggested repeating these stories in my mind over and over again and to share them with others. I could also put props up to remind me of those wonderful times. This practice helped make the happier memories bigger in my brain.

Using this idea, I thought: How could I make the gratitude feeling deeper and bigger?

A few years ago, upon waking up and before going to sleep, I would mentally list things I was grateful for. Many times, I noticed that I got distracted and did not get very far; or I would forget.

I put props in my room to remind me. For example, one of the first things I see when I open my eyes is an empty bowl. The Tibetan monks bring an empty bowl to their morning meditation, trusting that the bowl will be filled by the end of the day with the things that they need. No matter how the day goes, there is always something that gets put in the bowl.

I did begin to experience joy on occasion, although I generally still felt somewhat flat. Even though I still knew how tremendously lucky I was, that bubbling joy was still hiding from me.

To further the list of things I was grateful for, I began a small gratitude journal. Actually, it is a very tiny journal. My belief is, if it is small, it will take little effort, and I will be more likely to do it.

So, every morning upon waking, I would fill a tiny page, in point form, of things I was grateful for. For example:

- Waking up
- My body
- My bed
- The new day
- My children
- My pets
- Morning coffee
- A phone
- Good dreams
- Faith
- Trust

It did not matter if I repeated myself day after day, or how big or small these things were. I made no judgment. I liked how this felt, so I wrote a list in the evening, too, before sleep. Because the journal was tiny, it also could travel easily with me. I kept it up, and, after a few months, I noticed that I was waking up with a smile on my face and going to sleep with a smile on my face. I used to suffer from insomnia, now I sleep very solidly most nights. I like that.

After about a year, I was wondering how I could further expand my positive experience of gratitude and joy to ripple throughout the day.

So I began pausing as I was writing my gratitude list, letting the experience of what I was writing have a few more moments. I also began doodling little hearts and exclamation marks on the tiny pages. I pasted inspirational sayings into my journal. I also would look back at written pages and smile at my memory of events or listed items.

I noticed that a feeling of deep love and gratitude permeated my whole body. At first, it took me by surprise. A joyful feeling of excitement was dancing in my body. Then I realized I was finally expanding my inner joy to a point of ecstasy.

I began to see ways of self-love that I had not noticed before.

Smells, sounds, textures, tastes, fabrics, clothes, and pictures that brought joy became more evident.

Students and clients remark on how calm I am. I feel that I work hard on my inner stability. I also have worked on getting to know myself.

Sometimes I still have trouble filling out my gratitude journal. It might feel forced or flat. There might not be any obvious underlying reason for this. On those days, I read other pages until I find a page that makes me smile. And if reviewing pages does not work, I hum a song or two and usually that pulls me out of any dreary state.

My question is; how can I continue to support my calmness, my connectedness to life; how do I keep myself interested? *How do I keep the work fresh?*

One way I discovered was to make it more fun.

Fun things

Fun and enjoyable things are easier to do and keep doing. Life presents its own many and unpredictable challenges. Including fun things already makes us lighter and gives us something to look forward to in between periods of joy.

Picking one fun thing is enough to begin.

I like listening to **different speakers**; even though they might be sharing the same messages, their approach is unique and the brain hears the unique approach because it appears new.

I practise the law of attraction and goal structures. My daughter and I have a **vision board** in our kitchen that we modify regularly as wishes are manifested. Seeing my desires on the vision board is a way of getting my brain to recognize them and experience them.

I began to look around for practices that I hoped would help.

It was helpful for me to read various **spiritual materials** and **attend spiritual gatherings**. I noticed that when I began my day with some kind of positive inspirational spiritual reading, my thoughts were more positive throughout the day. I read and reread some of these books. Being around **like-minded people** feels good to me.

I access **daily inspirational quotes** that are free over the Internet. There are many to choose from with various themes. These inspirations begin a train of thought that guides my thinking in an inspired way.

I regularly use these quotes to create new **affirmations**. The word affirmation comes from the Latin *affirmare*, originally meaning "to make steady, strengthen." Affirmations are positive phrases that you create to describe how you want to be in your life.

They are very effective when practiced daily. This conditions our brain to adopt similar positive messages and ways of thinking. Our brain relates to what is familiar in our world. Even though an affirmation may feel false in the beginning, as your brain slowly relaxes into the familiarity of the positive message it begins to feel that it is possible and real.

Be very careful with your words, choosing to speak only those which work towards your wellbeing. Thoughts have power and energy.

When we change our thoughts, we restructure the neural pathways of our brain. When we think we are victims then that is what we will be. When we think we are creative then we are creative.

Affirmations do indeed strengthen our brain by helping it believe in the potential of an action we desire to manifest. When we write these same affirmations they become even stronger. Much like exercise, the more your exercise your brain, the stronger the muscle becomes. Like exercise the level of feel-good hormones rises and pushes our brain to form new clusters of positive thought and stronger neuropathways.

If you constantly say, "I can't," the energy of your words will indeed set you up to not be able. When you say, "I can!" the energy of your words will do just that!

Our thoughts translate into words. Eventually those words translate into actions.

Choose carefully the words that will help you to manifest your intentions.

Here are some of my favourite daily affirmations:

"This is the best day of my life!"

"I am content with the process."

"I am a channel of creative energy."

"All my needs are met."

"I am enough."

"All is well."

For more suggestions see the resources page at the back of this book, authors Florence Shinn and Louise Hay.

CREATIVE PRACTICE

Love List and Gratitude Journal

The following exercise has had a very positive impact on me and my students.

- Buy a small journal, lined or unlined.
- In the front of it, you might put some pictures or sayings that you find inspirational.
- Then every morning and night, list what you are grateful for, what warms your heart and makes you smile
- In the back, begin your list of your one hundred plus character qualities. You can get your friends and family to help. Creating this list may take a while; it may evolve over days and weeks. The result is that you begin to think better of yourself, and this reflects on how you view others. I transfer my list from my gratitude journal to the next journal and add to it regularly.
- Place it by your bedside with a pen or pencil, so at waking or going to bed, it is ready for you.
- You might add pictures or small mementos—for example, a ticket from a play or movie.

CREATIVE PRACTICE

Four hearts painting

Take a large piece of paper about 11 by17 inches or 18 by 24 inches, and draw on it four hearts with tempera paint or pastels. These hearts can be any size, shape, or colour.

One heart is the heart from one of your happiest times. Let the colours and shapes reflect that time.

One heart is the heart from one of the most painful times in your life. Again, let the colours and shapes reflect that time.

One heart is the heart that reflects your heart today. Again, let the colours and shapes reflect that time.

And one heart is the heart of the future. Again, let the colours and shapes reflect that time.

Before you set aside your paints, look at the hearts and describe them in terms of colours, dark, light, shades, strokes of lines, spaces, and texture.

When you are done, think about how these images reflect your heart throughout your life. Are there any surprises?

Does your heart of today and that of the future change at all? They may or may not.

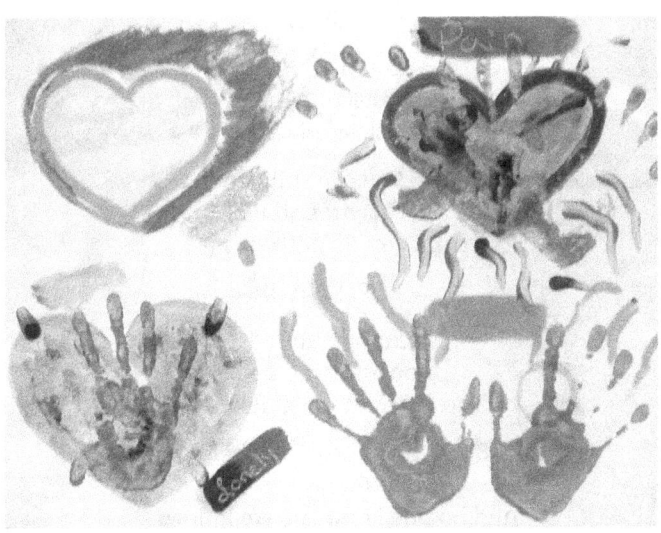

OUTER HAPPINESS

Are you living congruent with your beliefs?

The world outside of us is always changing. We do, however, have choices on how we shape and reshape some of our outside world to support more joy. This is accessible right now, with little change and little expense, if any.

Support your inner core from the outside by including more of your joys with your senses, your surroundings, what you put into your body and your body's condition. Some of these things intertwine between inner and outside worlds.

. . . So I looked at my outside world.

Ode to Umbrella

POP! SWISH!

A canopy unfolds,
sheltering me
during wet solemn journeys.

Outside is grey,
underneath you, a rainbow
that dances in my steps.

POP! SWISH!

A canopy unfolds,
protecting me
during sleet-driven cold.

Outside chill
swirls around us
and you do not waver.

POP! SWISH!

A canopy unfolds,
opening me up
to different possibilities.

Beginning above and below,
a breath goes free,
and no one knows where it flows.

ENVIRONMENT

I like a calm environment. I like my working space and home space to be my oasis. A place I can relax and be. Without judgment or pressure.

What is your oasis?

What would make it an oasis?

Cleaning up, sorting things, or having all your special things in one area . . . There are many ways to create your oasis. It just has to be one space or part of a space and does not need to be very big.

I began in my bedroom. I created a calm, serene place for myself. If it gets too cluttered, I can feel it and I sort it out again. I have been looking at my spaces differently and am in a constant process of calming them, for myself, my family, and my clients. Some of my spaces in my studio are very busy—I have included fun things in them. It gives my brain a visual relief.

Depending on where you live, you may need to go to a place in nature to create an oasis for yourself.

MUSIC, ENTERTAINMENT, READING

Years ago, I decided not to listen to the radio anymore and years before that, I stopped watching TV. More than the programs, it was the commercials that bothered me. I noticed that when I saw certain products in the grocery store, the jingles played in my head. I did not like that.

Everything we put into our brains influences us somehow. There is a Japanese philosophy that suggests that whatever we put into ourselves comes out again.

To the chagrin of some of my friends, I also don't watch the news and I don't read the major newspapers. If something big happens or is going to happen that affects me, I will tune in. I found long ago that the media is hugely inaccurate most of the time in sharing information.

I enjoy learning and studying about our world. I choose to do this in other ways. It's a balance—you need to find your own balance. Maybe you watch the news only once a day, or read one paper to stay in touch. Maybe this affects you less, as you may be more strongly balanced in another area.

Music and lyrics are important to me. I measurably limit music containing lyrics that are obsessively violent, self-pitying, and negative. Why do I want these thoughts humming around my head when that is not what I want or what I want to manifest in my life? Sometimes in theatre or arts collections, sadder pieces are part of the art. That is different than negative songs being repetitively played. For example, Fado, a soulful, melancholy, form of Portuguese folk music, is very lovely and mournful. It can be relaxing, quieting, and transformational, though maybe because I don't understand the language. Some operatic arias evoke strong emotions.

I use music to create and change moods for myself in my studio, in my workshops, and for my clients. Be aware of what you put in your environment. Most of the time, you have a choice. All these things are individual and affect us in varying ways.

CHOOSE AND DO WHAT WORKS BEST FOR YOU

Eckhart Tolle in *New Earth* shares three modalities of awakened doing: acceptance, enjoyment, and enthusiasm. Each in certain situations represents a different consciousness. I agree when he states that if you are not in one these states, you are somehow creating suffering for yourself and possibly others.

I'd like to present these to you in the context of creating more joy and peace in your life.

Acceptance

In a particular situation, you may or may not like a certain task, but you can do still do it willingly, or change how you do it. You might not like getting soaked in the rain or shovelling snow, but you can accept the task and be at peace with it.

I used to resist cleaning. Now, I see it as a way of loving my environments, whether gardening or making my bed. It is another way of loving my home, my family, and me.

Sometimes this state might appear passive; however, it really is transmitting a vibration of peace. If you really cannot accept or enjoy the task, then you must stop and take responsibility for your state of mind. Maybe it means changing the approach to the task or deferring it.

Enjoyment

When you enjoy what you are doing, it turns into a sense of aliveness. All of these states are states of being present. Usually when you are totally present, joy seems to creep into what you are doing, and there is a sense of mystery and aliveness. Enjoying what you do dramatically increases the quality of your life.

My clinical supervisor for my therapy practice says life need not be difficult, that we can do this life with ease.

Make a list of simple tasks such as driving, laundry, errands, or pouring a cup of coffee. Whenever you are involved in these tasks, there is an opportunity for alertness. You will discover that by being totally present in these tasks they will become enjoyable.

Enthusiasm

The third modality of awakened doing is enthusiasm. This happens when you are enjoying what you are doing and have purpose and vision for it. When you add this goal to the enjoyment of doing your task, it further heightens the vibration frequency and pleasure. This is the passion and thriving mode of living and loving your life.

If the goal becomes more important than the journey toward it, this desire creates stress. The ego says that focus and hard work will achieve your goals, and that creates tension as well. These stresses diminish both the quality and effectiveness of the energy in doing the task.

> **Being in the mode of enthusiasm all the time is not possible, but we can flow between the three modalities of acceptance, enjoyment, and enthusiasm.**

Self-care

Keeping a daily, regular practice of self-care is a way of maintaining well-being and thriving.

Breathing to harmony

Starting with the breath and slowing down leads one in a natural progression to harmony. The following chart, which has evolved over years of experience and facilitating workshops, illustrates the steps along the way. It also maps out our progress through this book, and can serve as a useful refresher down the road.

Harmony / peace / happiness / contentment / calm
↑
Global awareness
↑
Creativity / self-esteem / confidence / perception skills
↑
Self awareness / knowledge / imagination
↑
Process / learn
↑
Focus / concentrate
↑
Relax / silence
↑
Our source / our breath / proper breathing

Have you tried all the exercises? Try them on your own and with friends. Mix them up and combine them. Keep notes of your experiences so you can refer to them later. Consider your responses and benefits. Remember to be gentle with yourself. Consider references and other resources in areas that intrigue you, including those listed in the resources section at the end of the book.

We are born out of love

We are born creative

To be love

To be creative

To give love

To give creatively

It is with this love and creativity that we feel the most joy and harmony with ourselves, our lives, our partners, families, and the world.

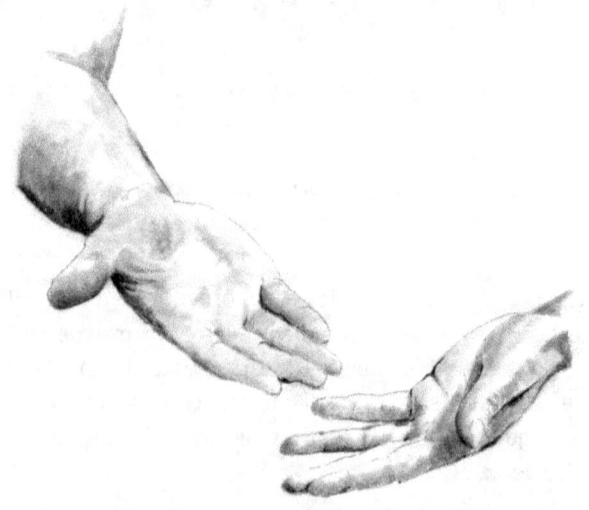

I hope you found a few treasures, a bit of wisdom, and a smile to ease your way.

RESOURCES AND REFERENCES

There are many wonderful books on the market to help us along our way. I have listed in the categories below a few titles that I use in my classes and that I have had personal success with. I am happy to share these titles with you.

Art

The following are great beginners' books and great support tools:

Brookes, Mona. *Drawing with Children.* Los Angeles, CA: Jermey P. Tarcher, Inc., 1986. A detailed manual and progressive workbook helping children to draw. Excellent tool for parents and teachers. Also, you can learn along with the children.

Edwards, Betty. *Drawing on the Artist Within.* New York, NY: Simon & Schuster, 1986. A book about understanding the artist within us.

———. *Drawing on the Right Side of the Brain.* New York, NY: Tacher/Perigee, 1989. A step-by-step book with exercises teaching the reader how to see and draw. Excellent guide.

Hawthorne, Mrs. Charles W., comp. *Hawthorne on Painting.* Toronto, ON: Dover Publications, 1960. Essays from Hawthorne and his workshops. This book encourages students in spontaneity, practice, and experience.

Creativity

Cameron, Julia. *The Artist's Way.* New York, NY: Tacher/Perigee, 1992. A twelve-week program to help readers discover their creative self and blocks. Lots of applications; best done with a buddy or in a group.

Dennison, Paul E., and Gail E. Dennison. *Brain Gym.* Ventura, CA: Edu-Kinesthetics, 1986. Many practical exercises to relax, rejuvenate, and stimulate brain activity.

Goldberg, Natalie. *Writing Down the Bones.* Boston, MA: Shambhala Press, 1986. All her books are excellent guides to stimulate the writer in you. Another way to self-discovery through writing.

Sobel, Elliot. *Wild Heart Dancing*. New York, NY: Fireside, 1987. A self-directed private creativity retreat. To be taken along and only read as you complete exercises. Lots of fun and worthwhile.

Emotions

There are many books on the market to help with emotional issues and questions. This is only a small selection of what is available. If you feel you want more, consider finding a counsellor to guide you more specifically.

Bassett, Lucinda. *From Panic to Power*. New York, NY: HarperCollins, 1997. Easy to read; author uses many of her personal experiences in a humorous way. Included are many support points for anxiety and worry.

Bilodeau, Lorraine. *The Anger Workbook*. Center City, MN: Hazelden Foundation, 1994. A simple workbook designed to get you thinking, understanding, and redirecting your frustration and angry feelings.

Brown, Brené. *The Gifts of Imperfection*. Center City, MN: Hazelden, 2010.

Pearson, Carol. *The Hero Within*. New York, NY: HarperCollins, 1991. Various human characteristics illustrated using hero characters.

Peck, M. Scott. *The Road Less Travelled*. New York, NY: Simon & Schuster, 1978.

Rosenberg, Marshall. *The Surprising Purpose of Anger*. Rosenberg won eleven peace awards for his work *Nonviolent Communication: A Language of Life*. There are many YouTube videos online and he has many small books explaining his model.

Expressive Arts

Allen, Pat B. *The Art of Knowing*. Boston, MA: Shambhala Publications Inc., 1995.

Atkins, Sally. *Sourcebook in Expressive Arts Therapy*. Boone, NC: Parkway Publishers Inc., 2007.

Knill, P., H.N. Barba, and M.N. Fuchs. *Minstrels of Soul: Intermodal Expressive Therapy*. Toronto: Palmerston Press, 2004.

Knill, P., E.G. Levine, and S. Levine. *Principles and Practice of Expressive Arts Therapy*. London, U.K.: Jessica Kingsley Publishers, 2005.

Kriz, Jurgen. *Self-Actualization*. Germany: Books on Demand, 2006.

McNiff, Shaun. *Integrating the Arts in Therapy*. Springfield, IL: Charles C. Thomas, 2009.

Rogers, Natalie. *The Creative Connections*. Palo Alto, CA: Science & Behaviour Books, Inc., 1993.

Spirituality

There are many spiritual books available. The following might supplement or offer alternatives to what you already have.

A Course in Miracles. New York, NY: Viking, 1996. A non-denominational book on God, Jesus, and living. A very heavy book, best studied with groups.

Dispenza, Joe. *You are the Placebo*. Carlsbad, CA: Hay House, 2014. This book is about you making your mind matter in creating your health and your life. It is backed with science and a team of doctors.

Ikeda, Daisaku. *Faith into Action*. Santa Monica, CA: World Tribune Press, 1999. A collection containing reflections for many life situations. Based on a Buddhist perspective.

Gray, John. *Practical Miracles for Mars & Venus*. New York, NY: Harper Collins, 1999.

Hay, Louise. *You Can Heal Your Life*. Carlsbad, CA: Hay House, 1999.

Heath, Yvonne, *Love Your Life to Death: How to Plan and Prepare for End of Life so You Can Live Fully Now*. Port Sydney, ON, 2015

Kavelin Popov, Linda. *The Family Virtues Guide*. New York, NY: Plume Books, Penguin Group, 1997. A basic book about morals and character.

Tolle, Eckhart. *A New Earth: Awakening to Your Life's Purpose*. New York, NY: Plume Books, Penguin Group, 2006.

———. *The Power of Now*. Vancouver, BC: Namaste Publishing, 1997.

Other references

Allen, James. *As a Man Thinketh*. New York, NY: Thomas Y. Crowell Co., 1902.

Attwood, Janet, and Chris Attwood. *The Passion Test: The Effortless Path to Discovering Your Life Purpose.* New York, NY: Penguin Books, 2007.

Benson, Herbert. *The Relaxation Response.* New York, NY: William Morrow and Company, 1975.

Buettner, Dan. *The Blue Zones, Lessons for Living Longer from the People Who've Lived the Longest.* Washington DC: National Geographic Society, 2008.

Byock, Ira, M.D. *Dying Well: Peace and Possibilities at the End of Life.* New York, NY: Penguin Pitman, 1997.

Campbell, Don. *The Mozart Effect.* New York, NY: Avon Books, 1997.

Canfield, Jack. *The Success Principles.* New York, NY: HarperCollins, 2007.

DeVita-Raeburn, Elizabeth. *The Empty Room: Understanding Sibling Loss.* New York, NY: Scribner, 2004.

Doidage, Norman. *The Brain That Changes Itself.* New York, NY: Penguin Books, 2007.

Doka, Kenneth. *Living with Grief.* 2000.

Franck, Frederick. *The Zen of Seeing.* New York, NY: Random House, 1973.

Frankl, Victor. *Man's Search for Meaning.* New York, NY: Washington Square Press, 1984.

Gawain, Shakti. *Creative Visualization: Meditations.* Novato, CA: New World Library, 1995.

Goldstein, Nathan. *The Art of Responsive Drawing.* Upper Saddle River, NJ: Prentice Hall, 1973.

Goleman, David. *Emotional Intelligence.* New York, NY: Bantam, 1995.

Hart, Mickey, with Jay Stevens. *Drumming at the Edge of Magic.* San Francisco, CA: Harper, 1960.

Jenkinson, Stephen. *How It Could All Be: A Work Book for Dying People and for Those That Love Them.* Victoria, BC: First Choice Books, 2009.

Liedloff, Jean. *The Continuum Concept.* Reading, MA: Addison-Wesley Publication Co. Inc., 1985.

May, Rollo. *The Courage to Create.* New York, NY: W.W. Norton, 1975.

Murdock, Maureen. *Spinning Inward: Guided Imagery for Children* for Learning, Creativity and Relaxation. Boston, MA: Shambhala Publications, 1987.

Nicolaides, Kimon. *The Natural Way to Draw.* Boston, MA: Houghton Mifflin Company, 1969.

Orlick, Terry. *Feeling Great: Teaching Children to Excel at Living.* Carp, ON: Creative Bound, Inc., 1996.

Pearce, Joseph. *Magical Child.* New York, NY: Penguin Group, 1997.

Pitman, Walter. *Making the Case for Arts Education.* Toronto, ON: Ontario Arts Council, 1997.

Roth, Gabrielle. *Maps to Ecstasy: Teachings of an Urban Shaman.* San Rafael, CA: New World Library, 1989.

Shinn, Florence. *The Game of Life.* Essex, U.K.: L.N. Fowler & Co., 1989.

———. *Your Word Is Your Wand.* Essex, U.K.: L.N. Fowler & Co., 1989.

Silberstein–Storfer, Muriel, and Mablen Jones. *Doing Art Together.* New York, NY: Harry N. Abrams, Inc., 1997.

Tavris, Carol. Anger: *The Misunderstood Emotion.* New York, NY: Simon and Schuster, 1982.

Von Oech, Roger. *A Whack on the Side of the Head.* New York, NY: Warner Books, 1998.

Wolfelt, Alan. *A Child's View of Grief.* Bozeman, MT: Companion Press, 1991.

Zukav, Gary. *The Seat of the Soul.* Boston, MA: Shambhala, 1991.

"If I have made your journey a little bit happier, then I have fulfilled my purpose."

ABOUT THE AUTHOR

Elke Scholz, MA, RP, REACE, is a well-known author, therapist, speaker, and facilitator. She was awarded a Masters degree in Expressive Arts Therapy by European Graduate School (EGS), Saas Fee, Switzerland. She is internationally certified in EMDR and is a registered expressive arts consultant/educator (REACE) with the International Expressive Arts Therapy Association (IEATA).

All her life, Elke has understood the connection between the arts and living. For her, the elements connect at every level, and she is able to simplify concepts and relay this to other people in a simple, approachable way. Elke communicates this understanding, as well as her own artistic vision, in numerous ways.

Elke has been helping people since 1980. Her calm approach invites a comfortable space for people to try new things. Elke can be with clients in their darkest, hardest times. Her acute awareness and high sensitivity are tremendous assets for her clients and make her distinctive in her field. Elke works well with teams of educators, social workers, doctors, corporations, organizations, and groups. Other facilitators immensely enjoy her training sessions.

Programs for Youth

Most of Elke's program development work focuses on attachment, grief, trauma, and loss recovery using Expressive Arts. She successfully manages her own anxiety and gladly shares her success strategies. Elke's focus is on building the strengths of young people. She facilitates youth grief and loss recovery programs that she designed and developed for a regional hospice in Muskoka, Ontario. This program continues to be extremely successful in helping youth and their families to cope with their grief and trauma.

Other group programs, which she facilitates in schools, are successful in assisting youth-at-risk with creative living and learning to become re-engaged with life, with attending class, and gaining life skills. Proceeds of this edition go towards these programs.

Frame of Reference

- Curiosity
- Mystery
- Discovery
- Guidance
- Leadershipg
- Non-positional, flexible, client-centred solutions

Elke's Own Creative Daily Principles and Practices

- Daily gratitude journalling, morning and evening
- Long meditative walks through nature
- Joyfully hand-raising chickens, as egg layers, therapy aids, and entertainment
- Writing poetry
- Community drumming workshops
- Learning to play the flute and the piano
- Hiking, mountain biking, kayaking, and sketching in the great, wondrous outdoors
- Inspirational reading
- Exploring philosophy and spirituality with different local discussion groups
- Exploring life, love, and the universe
- Expressing it all in painting and sketches

Please write to the publisher to let Elke know how this book works for you, or what you would like to see added to future editions.

The Artist's Reply
1060 Partridge Lane, Bracebridge, ON P1L 1W8
Tel: 705-646-2300   Email: elkescholz@theartistsreply.com

Visit *www.elkescholz.com*:
Free downloads, posters, radio talks, YouTube videos, and many more resources.

To book Elke for speaking engagements and workshops:
Tel: 705.646.2300   Email: elkescholz@theartistsreply.com

Available in Print and Ebook Format
online or inquire at your local bookstore

ORDER MORE COPIES

Loving Your Life, 3rd ed.

The third addition of this award-winning book with a foreword by Kate Donohue, a grandmother of EXA. Explore your creative mindfulness in this expressive arts book. Use it for daily inspirations, creative exercises and practices, for personal use, and in workshops. It is a fun and refreshing practical approach for well-being and for coming back to who you are.

SPRING 2017 RELEASE

Anxiety Warrior

This practical resource book is full of strategies and skills to manage and overcome anxiety. This book would have saved me a lot of pain if I'd had it in the past. Along with myself, there are five contributors. They are published authors, key note speakers, leaders and they are all professionals who are passionate about their work and empowering people

---

Also available from The Artist's Reply
1060 Partridge Lane, Bracebridge, ON P1L 1W8
Tel: 705-646-2300   elkescholz@theartistsreply.com

"Loving My Life" Journal

Journaling is a valuable activity that changes the neural pathways in our brain. Writing "it" down is a way to lessening our burdens. There is much research backing up the benefits of journaling. This journal provides 27 ideas to help initiate some personal exploration. Try, explore and play. Discover the ones you like and the ones that give you the most energy.